"*The Elephant in My Living Room* is an inspiring account of the power of God to heal and restore to wholeness. It effectively reminds us that no tragedy is beyond the reach of God's loving arms." —*Dick Lee, program manager, WCRF Christian radio*

"The one thing that propels Marlane's book into the exceptional category is that the story is from her heart. She makes it come to life with refreshing detail and complete transparency. A must read for anyone facing a persistent struggle of any kind." —*André Bernier, T.V. meteorologist, Cleveland, OH*

"After reading Marlane Renner's *The Elephant in My Living Room*, I was left with one overriding thought: courage! This is clearly a courageous book, about a courageous journey, written by a courageous woman, following a courageous Savior. I would recommend this book to anyone who wants to understand how the truth and love we have in God and others can become powerful tools for healing and wholeness." —*Jamie Rasmussen, Senior Pastor, OH*

"This is a riveting story that any wounded, struggling heart will readily identify with and find enlightening, encouraging, and energizing." —*Lud Golz, Minister at Large, OH*

"*The Elephant in My Living Room* is fascinating—we can see ourselves in many of the author's words." —*M.B.*

"I knew immediately that this was not an ordinary book. I could feel God's presence even in the early pages...I kept stopping and writing my thoughts and feelings...I was

'talking to God' about things I had not thought of for many years. Thank you, Marlane, for making this possible."
—D.F

"A book of triumph over tragedy, of forgiveness over bitterness, of the ultimate victory of Christ. It is a journey out of a prison...into a world of freedom and release."
—A.V.

"The beautiful and sometimes painful and pain-filled words and insights touched me so deeply. They gave me a glimpse of my own 'elephants' and helped me see that only with Christ can I ever do anything more than just hide them. (Of course, they aren't really hidden all that well except maybe from me! The thunder of that pachyderm is always there trumpeting its place and forcing me to look away.)" —P.W.

"After reading *The Elephant in My Living Room,* I was reminded that no one escapes the pains of life, but that with the Bible and knowing that the Lord is always with you, you can rise above any obstacle. Through this book, I have been lifted on high from my own traumas and demons to a place that allows me to live as God intended, with love, faith and forgiveness. The only elephants I see now are in the zoo, and I rejoice in them." —G.B.

"*The Elephant in My Living Room* is a book of hope...[it] will guide you from the depth of darkness to the shining light of freedom and love of God through the grace of Jesus Christ Himself!" —T.S.

THE ELEPHANT IN MY LIVING ROOM

Marlane Zillmann Renner

Evergreen
PRESS

ISBN 1-58169-110-6
For Worldwide Distribution
Printed in the U.S.A.

Evergreen Press
P.O. Box 91011 • Mobile, AL 36691
800-367-8203

TABLE OF CONTENTS

PREFACE

The Elephant in My Living Room, first birthed in 1994, evolved in a most amazing way. After befriending a desperate, hurting woman on a cruise ship while my husband and I were on vacation, I ministered to her emotional and spiritual needs, bid her adieu, and never thought our paths would cross again. Months later, to my surprise, I received a phone call from this new acquaintance. She invited me, a virtual stranger, to come to her beautiful Florida home and house-sit for three weeks while she toured Europe. Little did she realize God's hand in her invitation!

I had experienced an emotional healing earlier that same year and strongly desired to write a message of encouragement to others who are hurting. I desperately struggled to find the time and quietude necessary to write because of the incessant phone calls and myriad activities constantly crowding my life. God sovereignly knew that I needed to be sent a thousand miles away to a town where I knew no one and would have no interruptions. After consenting to this unusual invitation, I suddenly recognized it as His provision: a quiet, isolated venue for writing the story about the menacing "elephant" that plagued me for more than 28 years.

What is an "elephant in a living room"? It is something that is extremely obvious to others, but not to the person who entertains it. It's so big it affects everything—even one's thought process—and it prevents the individual from experiencing a free, joyful, and victorious life.

In two and a half weeks I produced the first version of *The Elephant in My Living Room* and then excitedly set about finding a publisher. Being a first-time author, I naively expected instant success. With each rejection I grew increasingly more frustrated and eventually set the project on the back burner of my priorities.

Months melted into years. Hundreds of people, after reading my initial manuscript, told me how powerful, meaningful, and helpful it was in identifying the "elephants" in their lives and providing a blueprint for healing. They encouraged me to persist in my endeavors.

Chief among my cheerleaders was my husband, Dan, who incessantly goaded me to complete what I had started. He told me, "You counsel people on a one-to-one basis using the book's healing principles but are able to help others only on a small scale. Just think, if you published your book, you could help people on a much grander scale. After all, that's why you want to publish it."

He was right and I knew it. Nonetheless, I procrastinated in picking up the manuscript to prepare it for publication until August 2001, nearly seven years after its inception. Those seven years overflowed with personal and relational growth experiences that drove me to my knees and into a deeper relationship with God.

When I was finally ready to tackle *The Elephant in My Living Room* once again, I was more spiritually prepared. Re-reading the original manuscript one hot, sticky, late-summer afternoon, I realized the writing lacked heart and emotional intensity. Though written in the first person, the book seemed impersonal. Manuscript #1, a skeleton, needed fleshing out. After seven years of living and maturing emotionally and spiritually, I finally mustered the courage to assess my true feelings and transparently transcribe them for others to experience. As with my emotional healing, this too was a slow, gradual process, requiring hundreds of hours of laborious work, but the final outcome was worth it.

I thank my loving, caring, and patient parents who

faithfully stood by me through my maturing process during my less-than-lovable years. Special thanks to my precious husband, Dan, who relentlessly encouraged me to share my story through the written word. I love you. Finally and most importantly, I thank my heavenly Father. Without Him, there would be no story.

CHAPTER 1

THE ELEPHANT IN MY LIVING ROOM

"Just trust me," he smiled. But something shifted behind his eyes.

"Just trust me," he said, unbuckling his belt and unzipping his pants.

"Just trust me," he grunted, as he covered my small body with his sweaty bulk.

I was an innocent child. He was 22 and weighed over 250 pounds. And he changed my life forever.

The story begins back in 1965 when I was 12 years old and the only daughter in a four-child household. I had always been a tomboy in many ways. Dressing dolls and playing house never had interested me when I was small; instead, I always preferred the outdoors, animals, and adventure. As a nine-year-old equestrian, I jumped and trained thoroughbred horses in Pittsburgh, Pennsylvania. I could experience no greater thrill than sailing over a four-foot fence on top of a two-thousand-pound steed. Horses were my life; I lived and breathed riding. I loved the smell of horse manure and horses' sweat, and at the end of a day of riding, I preferred my horsey-smelling clothes to a nightgown. That didn't go over well at all with my mother who forced me to strip off my pungent smelling riding habit in the basement before entering the main house. Although I protested, Mom was boss, so I followed her direction.

Disaster struck in the summer of 1965 when my father accepted a job offer in Cleveland, Ohio. This necessitated our moving. My life felt like it was over! I just knew that no place could be as nice as the cozy, hilly suburban community of Pleasant Hills, south of Pittsburgh. What was I going to do about my aspiring riding career? My world turned black.

To ease the pain of our move, my parents planned a six-week camping trip across the United States. My dad mixed business with pleasure as he prepared for his career change. Everything went extremely well until our ill-fated adventure on the stormy Outer Banks of Cape Hatteras, North Carolina.

My friend Susan, eleven at the time, joined us. We were complete opposites. Susan appeared older physically, though she was a year younger chronologically. I viewed guys as playmates; Susan saw them as conquests. I had never heard anything about the birds and the bees; she seemed to know all about them.

My parents, brothers, Susan and I loaded into our camping-gear-laden station wagon and headed towards our new destination, Cape Hatteras, with a sense of expectation. Little did we know what awaited us. The thousand-mile trek seemed interminable in the confining auto. We couldn't wait to pile out of our metal prison and dash for

2

the cool, refreshing ocean. Fat chance. As we approached the barrier island, the skies blackened, the winds increased, and before we knew what hit us, the unrelenting rage of a hurricane-intense nor'easter deluged us. Blinded by the torrent, we crept into the Buxton campground of the Cape Hatteras National Seashore. We arrived at our campsite only to discover we still had to remain inside the car. The hurricane-force winds rocked our vehicle back and forth as if a giant were using it as a plaything. Each time we tried to open the car doors, the force of nature slammed them shut on us. We were prisoners—seven claustrophobic, hungry, tired, weary vacationers in much need of a bathroom! Dinner consisted of warm bologna sandwiches and over-ripe bananas—a nauseating smell I vividly remember to this day. Forced to stay in upright positions, no one got a wink of shut-eye.

Morning finally dawned. After what seemed like eternity, the rains subsided, the winds abated, and seven grungy, cranky, starving passengers emerged from their cell. Totally disgruntled, I said, "Let's turn around and get out of here!" How I wished we had.

Mom suggested: "Let's just go for a little walk over the sand dunes and see the ocean. If you still want to leave, then we will."

It took just five minutes of walking on the beach before I changed my mind. The cool, moist sand under my feet and the salt spray caressing my face first softened my attitude. And when I observed the speedy sandpipers chase the outgoing waves in search of their morning meal, I couldn't help but fall in love with the place. We set up camp using the three-foot tent stakes previous Cape Hatteras campers had left behind and headed out to enjoy the pristine, sparsely populated beach. My vacation goal was to swim, exercise, and play with Susan and my brothers. On the other hand, Susan's was to flirt and pick up boys. She was a natural at it, while I didn't know the first thing about it.

Not long after her quest began, she met a guy about 14 years old, three years her senior, and seemed to hit it off with him, but I was too busy surfing to notice. When I finally emerged from the water to catch my breath before heading out again with my surfboard, Susan called me over and introduced me to her new-found friend. He mentioned he had an older brother he wanted me to meet. Totally naive and trusting, I said, "Sure!"

Herb, the older brother, arranged to come to our campsite that night and meet my parents. He arrived around seven, sat at the picnic table with my folks, and talked for a while before he asked if he could take me for a ride on the beach. His clean-cut demeanor and willingness to introduce himself to my parents led them to believe he was trustworthy and responsible. Therefore, they consented.

Leisurely cruising the beach, Herb and I witnessed a breathtaking sunset. Then he brought the car to a halt and suggested we get out and walk. Since I so loved walking barefoot on the beach, I concurred. Before we began our stroll, he opened the trunk and took out a blanket.

"What's that for?" I naively asked.

"It's in case we'd like to sit down on the wet sand."

"Oh, okay," I innocently agreed.

We walked for a while and conversed superficially as a typical 12-year-old would with an adult. Then Herb said, "Let's sit down here." Spreading the huge blanket onto the damp sand, we sat down and continued to talk for a few moments. All of a sudden Herb took half of the monstrous covering and started to engulf me with it like a tent.

Startled, I questioned him, "Why are you doing that?"

"It's so the mosquitoes don't get us." Since I absolutely loathe mosquitoes (because I'm usually the dinner for many of those nasty, blood-thirsty insects), I saw his logic and never disputed it.

My kind, caring new friend instantaneously transformed into a lion conquering its prey. Pinning me to the ground with his muscular frame, he started kissing me. Terror gripped me, and I commanded him to leave me alone, but he wouldn't relent. With every ounce of strength I could muster, I pushed against his steely torso and tried to escape from my adversary, all the while begging for an answer to my frantic question, "What are you doing?"

"Just trust me." With that, he unzipped his pants and pulled down my shorts.

Hysterical and confused, I shouted, "What are you doing?"

"I won't hurt you. Just trust me." Consumed by his own agenda, Herb ignored my pleas to stop, and the crash of the incoming waves on the shoreline covered my screams for help.

The rest is history. He sexually forced himself into me as I repeatedly, painfully pleaded for an answer: "What are you doing to me?" It hurt. Oh, did it hurt. The physical pain was excruciating, and the terror of helplessly being overpowered was overwhelming. But not understanding what he was actually doing to me terrified me most.

Then it was over. Dazed and numb, I lay on the blanket while he pulled up his pants and then redressed me. Loading the blanket and me into the car, he drove back to the campsite in silence. Without saying a word, he pulled into our campsite, opened the car door and let me out. Quickly he drove off into the darkness. Scared, confused, and not comprehending the life-changing impact of that innocent car ride, I stood there and watched him disappear into the inky blackness of the night.

My mom, who had just retired for the night, heard the car pull away and immediately called out to me, "Did you have a good time?" Still in shock, I could not answer. Sensing something wrong, she quickly emerged from the tent and reiterated, "Are you okay?"

I whispered, "I don't know."

"What happened? Tell me." As I replayed the sequence of events, Mom saw the terrified look in my eye and shrieked, "Oh, God!" She quickly roused my father and told him what happened. He dressed immediately and raced to the park ranger's booth to tell the ranger what had occurred. Sending a patrol car to Herb and his brother's campsite, the ranger discovered that they had pulled up stakes and fled. The ranger radioed back to the office and dispatched the police. The authorities pulled Herb's campsite registration card and checked his license plate number. They discovered he had used a pseudonym and a fake license number. Trying to track down the vehicle from my description, the police sent out an all-points bulletin to no avail.

What began as a joyous family outing turned into an emotional tragedy in one brief evening. Without explanation to my brothers or Susan, my parents broke camp the next morning and headed home to seek medical attention.

After the police and doctors did all they could regarding the matter, they sent me home to resume a normal life. Rape wasn't discussed openly in our society in 1965. My loving, caring parents, not knowing what follow-up measures to take, did nothing. They didn't tell my brothers of the incident and prayed that time alone would heal my physical and emotional wounds. Unfortunately, however, it didn't.

For the next 17 years a recurring nightmare plagued me as I relived the terror and helplessness of the rape. Many times I awoke in a cold sweat because it all seemed so real. The day God allowed this event to occur, the "elephant" walked into the living room of my life.

CHAPTER 2

YAHOO?!

Out of sight, out of mind. If it only were that simple, but it wasn't. The monstrous, unpredictable, emotionally destructive elephant resulting from the unresolved rape started affecting my life almost immediately, though no one noticed or at least admitted they did. Still an emotional youngster and therefore oblivious to the potential damaging effects of such a trauma, I didn't ask for help. My folks, naive as well, didn't attribute the changes in my personality to the Cape Hatteras incident. They assumed these were part of the natural growing pains of a pre-adolescent daughter. Thus, my unbridled emotional elephant subtly took up residence in my life.

Life was rough even without an invisible elephant. A new home, new town, and new school were a lot of changes for anyone; and unfortunately, I had to juggle them all at once. My family, despondent over leaving behind our beloved Pittsburgh and precious lifelong friends, half-heartedly got out of the car in the driveway of our new Ohio home near dusk the night before my first day of junior high school. Dad, trying to make the most of the difficult situation, dramatically opened the front door and flipped the light switch to illuminate our new living room, but nothing happened. We tried all the switches, but no lights came on in the living room, bedrooms, bathrooms, kitchen, or closets, even though the real estate agent had ordered the power to be connected the previous day. There we stood in the cavernous living room—six home-sick, hungry, weary, discouraged newcomers—as darkness rapidly approached. Dad set out to investigate the problem only to discover the previous owners had removed every light bulb from every socket in the house. Even worse, they had taken every roll of toilet paper! Helplessness and hopelessness overtook us, even my mom, who usually could find something positive in the most negative situations.

Just when everything seemed overwhelming, in came our savior. Our real estate agent—the only familiar face in town—rang the doorbell to welcome us to the community. He thought it strange to find us standing in darkness until he learned of our predicament. After assessing the problem, he excused himself, promised to quickly return, and disappeared. Thirty minutes later the doorbell sounded once again, and there stood our angel laden with bags of groceries that included lightbulbs and toilet paper. After first screwing in the lightbulbs, we voraciously con-sumed our supper of deli sandwiches, chips, and potato salad. With our stomachs satisfied, my brothers and I un-rolled our sleeping bags on the living room floor and at-tempted to get some much-needed rest before our first day of school.

There I lay on the living room floor in a new home, in a new town. No friends. Nothing familiar. Fear and anxiety nearly paralyzed me as I dreaded morning and the inevitable fate awaiting me—walking into a school filled with unfamiliar, judgmental faces. My mind reeled with "what ifs." *What if the kids didn't like me? What if I wasn't smart enough? What if I wasn't pretty enough?* The unending rhetorical questions plagued me.

Butterflies churned in my stomach as I stood in unfamiliar territory the next morning. Mom, my only friend, abandoned me following the school registration procedure.

"Have a great day," she called down the endless corridor as the guidance counselor escorted me to my first class. Would I ever see her again? I wasn't so sure.

I don't remember the specific events of that first academic day, but there's one thing I'll never forget—my long walk home. Since my parents hadn't had time to drive us around the neighborhood and acclimate us to our new surroundings prior to the start of school, I became hopelessly lost as I tried to make my way home. Anxiety over the day's activities magnified my already poor sense of direction. Alone, I aimlessly wandered the labyrinth of Bay Village streets looking for my new home. Minutes melted into hours. Nothing looked familiar. My legs ached; my heart pounded in panic. Tears welled up in my eyes as I repeatedly circled the blocks in vain. The third time I walked past a gardener manicuring her flowers, she sensed something terribly wrong and called out to me, "Are you lost? May I help you?" My panic began to subside at this glimmer of hope that I would finally be able to reach home. She asked for my school class schedule, read my home address on top of the paper, and gave me easy directions to follow. Within minutes I raced up the driveway and into the concerned, awaiting arms of my loving mother.

"Welcome home," she said. "How was your first day?"

"You don't want to know," I muttered through my tears.

Misery dominated my first month of life in Bay Village. I longed for my old life—my friends, my school, my horses. A creature of habit, I moped around the house lamenting my loss, resisting change, and wishing life could return to some semblance of normalcy.

"I hate this place! I want to move back to Pittsburgh," I complained to my mother.

"That's not an option, Marlane. Your father likes his new position. We're staying in Cleveland, so I suggest you open your mind, change your attitude, and focus on the benefits of living here."

I didn't like what Mom said one bit, but deep down I knew she was right. In time I lowered my defenses and opened my heart to Cleveland's potential opportunities.

NEW OPPORTUNITIES

With no English hunt seat equestrian riding venues on the west side of the city, my horseback riding career came to a screeching halt. My parents, desperate to find another athletic outlet for my pent-up energy, contacted the local YMCA. That one afternoon's inquiry opened doors of opportunity that significantly altered my future.

"Marlane, the Y has a swim team. Would you be interested in trying out?" Mom asked.

"I guess so. It couldn't hurt. At least it would be good exercise, and maybe I could meet some people."

Thus began my swimming career. During that first practice I eagerly crowded poolside with many other swim team hopefuls and waited for my chance to show the coach what I could do.

"Twelve-year-olds to the blocks," the coach barked. I nervously climbed the starting platform, curled my toes over the edge, adjusted my bathing cap, focused on my goal—the opposite wall 20 yards away—and anticipated the whistle. Seconds later I emerged first on the other end of the pool.

The coach, clipboard in hand, immediately approached me. "What did you say your name was? You're on the team." I had finally found my niche.

From that day until high school graduation, the Y became my home away from home. When not attending swim team practices, I lifeguarded, taught swimming lessons, and worked as a Y youth leader. Virtually every Saturday morning, blizzards notwithstanding, my parents sacrificed their precious sleep to get me to the Y for my 8:00 a.m. youth leadership training meeting. At that time, though, I never realized what a sacrifice it was on their part. As I committed myself to my volunteer efforts, my leadership skills and sense of responsibility increased, resulting in new respect from both peers and adults alike. Teamwise, I experienced success and respect as well. I took swim team practices seriously.

"If you don't feel physically ill after a workout, then you haven't pushed yourself enough," my coach once said. I worshiped my coach; consequently, I felt nauseated following most practices. The hard work paid off. My swimming skills, strength, and endurance increased over time, and regular first-place finishes in swim meets encouraged me to work even harder. I excitedly looked forward to the annual end-of-the-year banquets because I knew my efforts would be rewarded. Year after year I proudly accepted top honor awards in my age group division for Most

Yahoo!

Improved Swimmer and Most Valuable Swimmer. My peers
even elected me team captain. As I continued to excel in
competition, I won the coveted Cleveland All-City
Swimmer award. Unforgettable as these experiences were,
however, they pale in comparison to the memories in-
delibly cemented in my heart the day I heard my mom's
familiar "Yahoo" war whoop just seconds before com-
peting in the state swimming finals.

Giddy laughter masked tension as 30 sleepy-eyed com-
petitors hugged parents, received good luck wishes, and
boarded their streamer-bedecked bus bound for the state
capital. Mom never missed my meets. My best friend and
chief supporter, she cheered me on week after week,
month after month, year after year. Her famous piercing
"Yahoo" war whoop reverberated throughout many a
Cleveland natatorium, but the Columbus swimming venue
wouldn't hear her exhilarating cry since a packed team
bus precluded her from accompanying us on our journey.
The biting, pre-dawn March breeze nipped at our tear-
drenched cheeks as we waved good-bye to one another. It
wouldn't be the same without her.

My stomach churned throughout the seemingly interminable two-hour ride. Excitement mixed with fear, and
when the bus came to a halt, I anxiously exited and jogged
to the locker room to prepare. Waiting for a warm-up lane,
vainly gazing into the stands, I longed to see my mother's
familiar face, but no mom.

Unbeknownst to me, though, she had decided nothing
was going to prevent her from attending the meet. She
boarded a Greyhound bus scheduled to arrive in
Columbus just 20 minutes prior to the start of the YWCA
State Swim Meet. The timing was tight because ten blocks
separated the bus station from the swimming venue, and
the coach scheduled me to anchor the first event, the 200-

yard medley relay. She knew she just had to make it in time.

Nervous and distracted, I muttered through the singing of the national anthem, panned the bleachers one last time in search of my mom, and realized I was on my own.

"Two-hundred yard medley relay," called the announcer.

"Swimmers, take your mark." Bang! The gun echoed as the first swimmers smacked the water in a mad frenzy.

"Go, go, go!" I screamed to my teammate as she raced down the pool. Swimming freestyle, I competed last so when the butterflier entered the tension-filled water, I mounted the starting block and awaited my turn to make history.

"Yahoo!" shouted a familiar voice from the crowd. Distracted, I briefly turned to see my precious mother, who was heavily panting but proudly standing in the bleachers. Smiling ear to ear, she shouted, "Yahoo! Yahoo!" as the butterflier aggressively charged the wall. I don't remember even touching the water as I sprinted that last 50 yards to a first-place victory. Overall, our team finished third at state; I returned to Cleveland sporting three first-place medals and one second; and Mom kept her perfect attendance record intact.

Subsequent to this success, Olympic coaches came to our home and tried to persuade me to commit to a grueling training program in preparation for the upcoming Olympics. Feeling both flattered and deeply honored, I contemplated the sacrifice: four years living with a host family in either California or Texas, minimal quality family time, and the financial burdens on my family. My parents left the decision to me. Wrestling with the proposition, I painstakingly concluded I valued family and a well-rounded life more than the long shot of winning gold. Though I never regret turning down the opportunity, I admit I still vicariously swim my Olympic events every time I watch the summer games!

Where was the elephant in all of these positive activities: swim team member, swimming instructor, youth leader, life guard? Did the rape of the past impact this period of my life? Yes, although I denied it. Subconsciously fearful of male control, I used my Friday and Saturday night lifeguarding job as an excuse not to date. "After all, I am a responsible teenager and have a job in order to earn money for college," I rationalized. In reality, though, I purposely insulated myself from men, all of whom I considered potential rapists. "No one's going to hurt me again," I vowed.

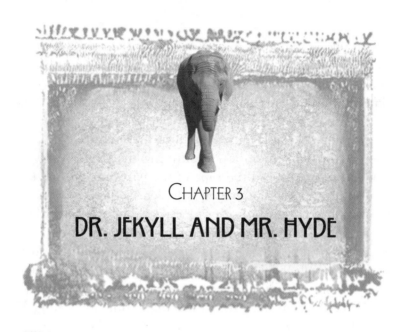

CHAPTER 3

DR. JEKYLL AND MR. HYDE

The Cape Hatteras horror greatly affected my attitude towards men. Except for my three trustworthy brothers and Dad, my protector, I unconsciously lumped all males into the same sick stereotype—controlling, insensitive, overpowering liars—if they got too close to me. Therefore, I controlled each of my friendships with males by setting the boundaries of how far each could go. Unfortunately, on many occasions I inadvertently lowered my guard and allowed my male friends to cross that invisible line between my emotional safety and possible danger. My elephant immediately reared his ugly head, quickly and effectively squelching any potential wholesome male relationships. An involuntary, explosive, schizophrenic-like Dr. Jekyll/Mr. Hyde personality transformation took place that frightened even me.

I could count the sum total of all my high school dates on two fingers: the girl-ask-boy Snow Ball dance and the prom. Each experience proved safe since I handpicked my escorts. We ate, talked, and danced, but that was it. No other extracurricular activities occurred; I would not allow it. Though both dates secretly liked me, they wisely kept their emotions to themselves and so never experienced my Dr. Jekyll/Mr. Hyde transformation up close and personal. Since my only two dating ventures appeared successful, my parents, assuming I had outgrown my childhood trauma, sent me off to college to get an education and possibly meet my future spouse.

Like a child set free in a candy store, I overindulged in my social life during my freshman year. Every weekend I dated a different guy, thanks to the pictorial freshman baby book provided each Wittenberg student. When the phone rang and I recognized an unfamiliar voice asking me for a date, I stalled for time by initiating small talk. "Where's your home town? What classes are you taking this quarter? What's your major?" I nonchalantly asked. All the while, my heart pounding, my palms sweating, I feverishly paged through the photo book in an attempt to match a face with the voice and make a split-second decision whether or not to accept the invitation.

I loathed drinking, not so much because of the alcohol but because of the possible loss of control as a result. This unconscious fear, masked by a dislike for liquor, precluded me from personally experiencing the questionable thrills of inebriation. I specifically avoided most fraternity or sorority parties and guys who prided themselves on the number of beers they could consume. Instead, I gravitated to the academic, introverted, square guys on campus because they appeared more safe, innocent, and predictable.

I so appreciated my male buddies. In truth, I preferred male friendships to female ones. After all, guys thought

17

more logically, displayed less emotion, and acted less capriciously than women. Thus, juggling my sacred free time among three male companions, I enjoyed many a Wittenberg experience, from semester final midnight food fights to mud sliding through the center of campus on W Day. Relishing my uncomplicated, platonic male relationships, I spent more and more time with each of them, but such an increased time commitment sent false messages to them as to my emotional and romantic intentions. Each misread my interest in spending more time with him as my desire to graduate to boyfriend/girlfriend status. When they responded as any healthy adult male would, they weren't prepared for what ensued.

One wholesome relationship after another dissolved due to a natural progression of events: an innocent kiss on the cheek, a romantic kiss on the lips, an erotic hug. The unresolved emotional memories from the past instinctively flooded me, drowning any logical reasoning. I misinterpreted each of my male friend's innocent advances as another rape threat, and the Mr. Hyde within lashed out in erratic, venomous rage.

"Who do you think you are?" I would shout. "What do you think you're doing? You've ruined it all! Everything was going so well until now! I don't want to see you ever again!" Shocked and confused, each cautiously backed off and out of my life. The last thing these shell-shocked, quality individuals wanted was another confrontation with Mr. Hyde!

This unhealthy interaction with men continued throughout my Wittenberg years and into adulthood. Chronological maturity and a convincing social facade masked the emotional twelve-year-old child living within.

Every available spring break I'd return to Cleveland to

visit family and share the events of my college experience. Inevitably, my oldest brother Phil would broach the recurring subject of promising men in my life.

"Well, Sis, how is your love life?" he'd ask. "Anybody special?"

The names changed every spring break when we discussed this sensitive topic. Phil, quick-witted and sarcastic at times, often quipped, "What's wrong? Isn't anybody good enough for you?" Year after year I outwardly endured his innocuous verbal barbs, but inwardly they festered.

After I had been teaching for five years, Phil again broached the topic of my love life during a playful brother and sister conversation.

"Sis, who's the new man in your life now?" he teasingly queried.

"No one in particular."

"Sis, if you're not careful, you're going to end up as an old-maid school teacher!"

I could withhold my tongue no longer. Mr. Hyde angrily fired back, "Phil, how *can* you make these biting, hurtful remarks year after year, knowing what I experienced as a child?"

Ignorant of what had happened, he innocently responded, "What do you mean, Sis? What did you experience?"

"You don't know?"

"Know what?"

"I was raped by a stranger at the age of twelve!"

Phil's jaw dropped. Dumbfounded, humiliated, and guilt-ridden, he muttered, "I never knew. No one ever told me. If I'd known, I never would have kidded you like I did all of these years! I'm sorry." He immediately confronted my mother and angrily denounced her for not telling him or my brothers about the trauma. I never heard another disparaging comment about my single state after that day.

How did I escape the harmful Dr. Jekyll/Mr. Hyde personality syndrome and start to heal from the deleterious effects of the elephant in my living room? By meeting Someone who changed my life forever.

CHAPTER 4

THREE STRIKES AND YOU'RE IN!

One childlike heart's desire dominated my life—I wanted to be loved. As elementary as this sounds, I didn't experience the fulfillment of this need until I was 21.

As you have seen, I grew up in a loving family. My parents expressed their devotion to me in many ways. They provided a beautiful home in a safe, academically sound neighborhood, fed me nutritiously, clothed me adequately, and disciplined me fairly. They demonstrated their love the most, though, by prioritizing their time to accommodate my needs and interests.

As far back as I can remember, my parents wholeheartedly devoted themselves to my brothers and me. Though Dad traveled extensively during the week due to his job commitment, he took time during the weekends to involve himself in his children's activities. Family camping outings, scouting events, swim meets—he was always there for us. I fondly remember the frigid Saturday afternoons when Dad sacrificed the warmth of home to take us sledding. Piling on his back on top of the sled, we'd hold on for dear life as we sailed down the ice-packed hill. At the bottom, with our cheeks a bright red and our toes tingling, we'd zealously exclaim, "That was fun. Let's do it again!" to which untiring Dad rolled his eyes, smiled, grabbed the sled rope, and towed us up the hill for yet another chilling run.

More importantly, Dad taught my brothers and me the value of education by sharing his love for learning and reading. I vividly recall the early years of sitting on his lap and listening to him read *Born Free, Living Free*, or *Kon Tiki*. As he neared the end of an exciting chapter, I was engrossed in the plot and begged, "Just one more chapter, Daddy!" Getting a nod of approval from Mom, he'd continue his narration until I dozed off to sleep in his arms. Then he'd carry me to bed, tuck me in, and give me a good night kiss. I always knew Dad loved me.

Mom lived to love. She poured her heart and soul into my life and always made herself available both physically and emotionally. Not once throughout my entire school career did I come home to an empty house. I knew I could walk through the front door, yell "Hi, Mom!" and get a hearty response.

"Hi, sweetheart! How was your day? Tell me about it," she'd say. Then over homemade chocolate chip cookies or some other delectable morsel, I'd share the joys and trials of my day and eagerly await some tidbit of wisdom from my precious confidant and counselor.

Mom always made time for me. Never too busy to sew on a loose button, make a last-minute batch of cupcakes for a school party, or host a major bash following the annual choir musical, Mom involved herself in every possible activity. Subsequently, our home became the party center of the neighborhood. Firefly catching parties, birthday sleepovers, and homemade popsicles gave way to after-prom parties, pre-football game potlucks, and her famous flaming Baked Alaska. Nothing proved to be too much for Mom! She delighted in serving. Mom epitomized love.

DEALING WITH PHYSICAL LOVE

The Cape Hatteras nightmare had poisoned my pure, innocent attitude towards physical love. Prior to the incident, neither my parents nor my school teachers had engaged me in a discussion about sex; society mostly ignored the topic in the 60s. Surprisingly enough, subsequent to the incident still no one broached the subject with me. Living in continued ignorance, physically repulsed by what appeared to be an overpowering, irreverent act, and psychologically and emotionally scarred by the frightening trauma, I viewed sex and physical love as a disgusting, dirty, controlling, painful act. Tainted, I instinctively misinterpreted any male's physical embrace (except my dad's and brothers') as the preface for an imminent rape. A tug of war raged within my heart—there was the inborn desire to reach out, touch, and experience the warmth of physical love, yet at the same time, the fear of becoming a victim once again.

Love—what did that really mean? I wrestled with the conflicting ideas and desperately needed to embrace a pure role model of true love, one I finally found October 13, 1974.

KNOWING LOVE

I've always believed in God. Raised in the Lutheran

23

faith, I attended church from infancy. Sunday school, catechism, choir, vacation Bible school—I did it all. I memorized liturgies and rotely sang them week after week, year after year. Confirmation classes taught me about God's goodness and His love. I absorbed a lot of head knowledge about this God in whom I believed, but I didn't really *know* Him. I looked at God as an unapproachable, ethereal Creator of the universe who did a lot of good things in the past but wasn't relevant today. In essence, I put Him in a nice little box and placed Him, along with my dust-covered Bible, on an inconspicuous shelf of my life. No wonder I fell asleep during sermons and thought the Word was boring. Due to this arm's-length relationship with God, I didn't feel comfortable approaching Him with personal problems, and my shallow shopping-list prayers appeared to fall on deaf ears. God remained elusive. Something was missing, but I didn't understand what.

Upon graduation from high school, I enrolled in a four-year Lutheran college where I faithfully attended daily chapel services and weekly Sunday services. I caught up on much-needed sleep during the academic, esoteric sermons that I had difficulty understanding without a dictionary. I rejected invitations to campus Bible study fellowships because I thought I knew it all and didn't need them.

As emotional, academic, and relational problems arose during those college years, I initially called my personal counselor—Mom—long distance and discussed the crises with her. Upon opening my first phone bill, I realized I needed to change my problem-solving tactics, so I wrote letters to her instead. Many issues required rapid responses, however. Resistant to change, I begrudgingly assumed personal responsibility for my life, and through trial and error grew more confident in my decision-making ability. Severing the apron strings, though painful and uncomfortable, increased my emotional maturity.

Due to my distant relationship with God, I never really thought of asking His advice about difficult personal issues. He couldn't talk to me any way, so I didn't bother talking to Him.

In June 1972, Billy Graham visited Cleveland, and thousands packed the municipal stadium nightly to hear his evangelical message. Our local church, participating in the event, sent busloads of parishioners, young and old, and I joined them. Sitting in the Browns stadium critically listening to Dr. Graham's message, I evaluated his delivery more than his content. "It should be 'me' not 'I,'" I whispered to my grammatical genius dad sitting beside me. My rebellious spirit warred against what I was hearing.

"Jesus is the answer to all of your life's problems," Billy encouraged.

Then where was He that night in Cape Hatteras while that man raped me? Anger seethed behind my calm, unassuming facade.

"It's not about religion; it's about relationship," Billy instructed. "If you'd like to begin a personal relationship with Jesus Christ, make Him Lord and Savior of your life, and start developing an ongoing fellowship with Him, feel free to get out of your seat, come down onto the field, and someone will pray with you. You can begin this new relationship tonight. Don't wait."

My spirit witnessed to the truth of his words, but my intellect reminded me: *Remember the last time you relinquished control of your life to someone. Look what happened. What makes you think God is any different from the man who hurt you?*

Standing in the bleachers, tears rolling down my cheeks, I chokingly sang "Just As I Am" and "Amazing

Grace" as hundreds streamed onto the field for prayer. One by one my compatriots abandoned me, and soon I stood alone. Self-conscious, convicted, and still rebellious, I eventually joined the others on the stadium floor. Although orally committing myself to a new personal fellowship with the Lord, I inwardly feared change and giving up what was familiar. Though friends congratulated me on my new commitment to God, secretly I knew that I still sat on the throne of my life.

Two years elapsed. I attended church and Bible studies and tried hard to do what I thought was expected of me, but I still lacked peace, regardless of all my human efforts. There had to be something more. Though joyful on the outside, behind closed doors the hideous emotional elephant trampled my inner peace, combined the unresolved hurt of the past with current personal problems, and transformed me into an angry volcano. Unknown to others, this volatile, venomous personality dwelt within. Though dormant for months at a time, it eventually erupted and emotionally scarred my closest friends and family.

Nothing changed because I still hadn't entered into fellowship with the heavenly Father.

SOMETHING DIFFERENT

Spring break of 1974 I returned to Bay Village to visit family and friends. Something seemed different. I couldn't identify it, but I liked it. Mom's heart smiled; a peace and joy radiated warmth and a sense of contentment I'd never witnessed.

"What happened?" I curiously asked.

"Do you really want to know? Then come with me Sunday morning" was all she said. Early Sunday morning, not wanting to awaken the men, we tiptoed out of the house and headed to church, but, surprisingly, not the church I normally attended in Bay.

"Where are we going?"

"You'll see."

Entering the crowded parking lot, I heard lively, joyous singing and curiously headed for the closest church entrance. I emerged nearly an hour and a half later, though it seemed as if only minutes had elapsed. I felt different: energized, encouraged, and uplifted. The minister's words burned in my spirit. I knew I'd heard this message before. Then I remembered Billy Graham.

"That's what happened," beamed Mom.

NEW LIFE BEGINS

In September 1974 I returned to Wittenberg University to complete my senior year. Little did I know what awaited me—an evening that transformed my life forever.

Maranatha, a Christian band, performed on campus October 13. Sitting in the crowd, I again experienced the message of joy, peace, and hope shared at the Billy Graham crusade and my mom's new church. For the third time my spirit burned and testified to the message's truth. This time I responded differently. Repentant tears cascaded my cheeks as I sincerely bowed in humility, wholeheartedly placed my faith in the Lord, and willingly entered into what became an ongoing fellowship and walk with Him.

My subsequent baptism testified of the life-changing decision to follow God unwaveringly, trust Him completely, and serve Him tirelessly. I've never regretted my decision. On October 13, 1974, I understood the true meaning of love for the first time.

CHAPTER 5

HIS WILL, NOT MINE

ollowing the change in my heart, I expected miracles—the death of my emotional elephant, no more erratic temper tantrums, no more relational problems, just peace, happiness, and joy. I secretly wished away the control issue I had battled since 1965 and thought my actions and desires would now magically conform to God's perfect plan for my life. Therefore, without consulting the One to whom I recently dedicated my future, I boldly, confidently, and defiantly set out to choose my life career. Without His subtle, loving guidance and divine timing, I could easily have settled for second best.

FINDING MY PURPOSE

God created human beings for a purpose. I understand now that I was born to teach. My teaching career commenced at the age of seven when I tutored a German teenager who was visiting our home for a year. A second-grade student during the day, I reversed roles in the evening and taught English to Margaret, our live-in European guest. Sitting on the basement steps, Margaret recited English grammar rules I had learned just hours before in my elementary school class. Duplicate handouts, requested from my second-grade teacher, aided in Margaret's learning process.

"'I' before 'e' except after 'c,' or when sounded as 'a' as in neighbor or weigh," I drilled into Margaret's German-thinking brain.

"The English language is very difficult," I encouraged Margaret, ten years my elder. "For every grammar rule there's an exception to the rule. It takes time, but with hard work you'll learn." And learn she did. Dad hung blackboards on the basement walls that we used for drilling vocabulary, spelling, and arithmetic. He also provided a file cabinet that I promptly filled with handouts and exercise worksheets needed for my classes. In no time, attendance expanded from a class of one to a class of a half-dozen as other neighborhood children gravitated to the Zillmann basement stairs to play school. I took this game seriously!

My teaching career continued at the local YMCA. For six years I instructed students, both young and old, in the intricate skills of swimming. Back float, dead man's float, breast stroke, rotary breathing, butterfly, flip turns—whatever the level of skill difficulty, I taught it. Studying a student's ineffective stroke, I had the gift of not only discerning the problem but clearly communicating it to the individual so he could correct it.

Once again I taught people many times my senior. One student in particular was the high school head football and wrestling coach. Though athletically gifted in many other

29

areas, Coach couldn't swim. He couldn't even float because negative buoyancy plagued him. Like a rock, he sank no matter what floating techniques he executed. Needless to say, Coach challenged my teaching skills to the maximum!

After entering college, I began seriously contemplating my future. What would I do with my life? Friends and family assumed I'd teach. Still wrestling with control issues, I adamantly announced, "Maybe I don't want to teach. Nonetheless, I'll get my teaching certificate just in case I want to fall back on it."

That's just what I did. I declared a speech/theater major with certification to teach. In spring of my senior year, just eight weeks prior to graduation, Xerox was looking for sales people and interviewed seniors on campus. Three other students and I received job offers. *Earning some serious money, I'll be successful,* I concluded.

Days later Xerox contracts arrived in the mail for the three other students. Staring into my empty mailbox, I wondered whether the post office lost my contract. A call to Xerox assured me that my job offer was in the mail. That same day, Mayfield High School called my Wittenberg residence.

"Marlane Zillmann, we're interested in hiring you to coach our men's swim team and teach high school English. When can you come to Cleveland for an interview?"

My mind reeled. Questions and random thoughts bombarded my brain. *I never applied to Mayfield High School. Where was it located anyway?* If I taught, I decided I'd only teach on the west side of Cleveland. *How in the world did they get my name?*

"I have a job pending, but I haven't signed a contract yet. My major is speech/theater, not English. I currently am four courses shy of a certification in English, and I only have eight weeks before I graduate."

"No problem," the caller responded. "Can you arrange to interview with us this Thursday around 11 a.m.?"

Without thinking I said, "Sure. How do I get to your school?"

"It's located on Cleveland's east side."

That's a different country, I thought, as I reached for scrap paper and haphazardly scribbled directions. Ending the call, I stood numb and speechless by my desk.

"What was that all about?" my college roommate inquired.

"You won't believe this!" was all I uttered.

Mom, my cheerleader and navigator, drove with me to the interview. What transpired was nothing short of miraculous. In less than an hour I met with the school principal, English department head, speech department head, athletic director, and former head swim team coach. When I reported back to the main office, the secretary instructed me to get a bite to eat and report to the superintendent's office at one o'clock sharp.

Lunch was a blur. At precisely 1:00 p.m. the superintendent's secretary ushered me into her superior's foreboding, massive office.

"What would you say if I offered you a contract to teach English and coach men's swimming?" the Mayfield district chief asked.

Appearing calm, I responded, "That would be very nice." I could barely control myself. My spirit confirmed this as God's choice for my life, and my heart screamed a big "Yahoo!" Affixing my John Hancock to the contract, I knew this was the right decision.

31

The superintendent, congratulating me on my new career, proudly stated, "You're very fortunate to get a job in the Mayfield School District."

Smiling, my mom confidently replied, "No, it's you who are fortunate!"

GOD'S PERFECT TIMING

I returned to Wittenberg on Friday morning to discover the Xerox contract awaiting me, one day too late. Looking back, I recognize God's perfect timing. Not only did He slam shut the Xerox door of opportunity, but He opened wide the teaching door. By summer's end I completed the required coursework for English certification, and in the fall of 1975 I established permanent residency on Cleveland's east side. Despite my prideful stubbornness, God sovereignly led me into the career in which He had gifted me. He knew I was born to teach; after all, He created me.

CHAPTER 6
HOOVER

I love to eat. I always have. Unlike some people, whatever I eat, I become, for better or worse. Though as a child I escaped my familial tendency towards obesity due to an active life during my tomboy years, age took its toll. Childhood was forgiving. I ate thousands of calories per day in my developmental years and still maintained the appropriate weight for my age and body frame. Growing up with three brothers, many times I felt like one of the guys, and at the dinner table I ate like one. My oldest brother, Phil, nicknamed me Hoover because he said when I ate I reminded him of our vacuum cleaner—I sucked up everything in sight. Remembering the starving children in China, I made sure to finish every last speck of food on my plate each and every meal. A regular member of the Clean Plate Club, I only remember once when I didn't ravenously gobble up everything put before me— the night Mom served liver and onions. Normally I liked her liver and onions, but for some reason this particular evening I couldn't stomach the thought of eating it. I gagged on the first bite, and for one hour, sitting tableside, I refused to eat another. Finally I offered what I thought a viable solution: "How about we get a shoe box and send my dinner to the starving kids in China. It would be good for them." Needless to say, we never sent the shoe box, and possibly for the first time in my young life, I experienced hunger pangs when I went to bed that dinnerless night.

ROLLER COASTER STRUGGLE

The onset of puberty, exacerbated by the rape trauma, marked the beginning of an on-going roller-coaster struggle with weight. I subtly started gaining weight, although my parents and I attributed it to puberty. My teen activities, especially swimming, masked my underlying weight problem, and not until college did it surface.

During freshman and sophomore years when I lived in the dorm, I subscribed to the all-you-can-eat college food plan—literally! Frugal, I wanted to get my money's worth, and that I did. Walking through the cafeteria line day after day, I piled high my calorie-rich/ health-food-poor tray and promptly headed for an unobtrusive cafeteria corner to voraciously devour it. The deeply ingrained clean plate mentality goaded me to finish every last bite, even if it meant overeating.

This time, though, I paid the hefty price for my overindulgence. Less physically active, due to my heavy college academic schedule, I nonetheless maintained my childhood eating habits. In no time, my jeans seemed to shrink as my weight increased. On winter break, Phil welcomed me home, gave me the once over, and promptly re-named me "chipmunk cheeks." Thus began a vicious, debilitating cycle: I ate; I gained weight; then I hated myself for gaining weight; and out of frustration, I ate even more.

Subconsciously, my weight gain served a purpose: I used it as a defense mechanism to protect myself from intimacy with men. Brainwashed by the media, I bought the lie that "thin was in." Hoping men preferred women 100 pounds wringing wet, I figured my extra weight would safeguard me from another emotional rape trauma.

I graduated from college wearing a size 14 dress, almost double my high school size. Fortunately, my height and body frame fooled people into thinking I weighed less than the scale testified. Though no one ever called me fat, I once overheard my mother describe me as matronly. That word stung because I had always reserved it for older women, certainly not 22-year-olds fresh out of college. In truth, the weight aged me, and as I began my first year of teaching, I didn't look like the rookie I was.

I entered the professional work world carrying all of the unresolved emotional baggage of the past. Although I now had a relationship with the Lord, I still struggled. It was difficult to balance my personal life with all of my new career responsibilities. Many times I faltered and often doubted the wisdom of my career choice.

One morning, sitting in the teachers' lounge and drowning under a mountain of essays, I lamented my plight and verbalized my heart thoughts: "Maybe I made a mistake accepting this teaching and coaching job. That sales position with Xerox looks mighty inviting right now."

A seasoned instructor, recalling her initial teaching experience, exclaimed: "Didn't anybody warn you? The first year of teaching is hell. Get used to it. If you survive this, you're home free. Hang in there."

I survived, one day at a time: up at 5:30 a.m., to school

by 7:00 a.m., swim team practice after school till 7:00 p.m., dinner, lesson plans, paper grading, swim team strategizing till midnight, in bed by 12:30 a.m.

"TGIF!" I shouted, bounding for my getaway car on Friday afternoons. The year couldn't end fast enough.

Compounding the already difficult teaching and coaching schedule was my living accommodation. Renting a room from a recently divorced elderly woman, I faced another challenge: the homeowner forbade me kitchen privileges. With no refrigeration and only a warming hot plate, I reverted to unhealthy eating habits to quell my hunger pangs. Homecooked meals consisted of donuts, instant coffee, pop tarts, and canned chunky soup. My scale groaned as my dress size increased to 16.

Just when I couldn't stand the thought of consuming another can of chunky soup, a friend and fellow swim coach invited me to his apartment for a home-cooked meal. Thus began an on-going ritual that not only ministered to my physical needs but my emotional needs as well. Bruce, a veteran teacher and coach, prepared sumptuous, healthy meals in his kitchen while I sat in the living room grading English papers or preparing swim meet lineups. During dinner he empathetically listened while I bitterly complained about the teachers who sat in the teachers' lounge day after day reading the newspaper while I slaved over stacks and stacks of papers. After I vented my numerous frustrations, with a twinkle in his eye, he'd finally respond, "Mar, there's an easy solution to your problem. Don't give your students so much work!"

Bruce knew me well, so he was well aware of my total commitment to teaching and to my students. He knew that many hours of paper grading accompanied that commitment, but he also knew I needed to play every once in a while so I wouldn't burn out before the year ended. He'd sensitively plan elegant dinner and theater getaways to break the monotony of school. Aware of my paper load, he invited me to bring my stacks of compositions along on the date so I could continue to grade them until we pulled into the restaurant or theater parking lot. A dedicated teacher himself, he understood me and unconsciously committed himself to helping me survive that maiden year.

I considered Bruce my best friend, and food my next best friend. Food rewarded me for those interminable marathon paper-grading evenings and made my work more palatable. Armed with my arsenal—a tapestry bag of English compositions, red pen, dictionary, grammar book, large jar of chunky peanut butter, bag of chocolate chip morsels, and a soup spoon—I jumped into bed, propped my pillows, nestled under the covers, adjusted the light, and zealously dove into the overwhelming stack of papers. Undaunted, I knew that 35 papers later I'd earn my first of five rewards: a heaping spoonful of peanut butter bedecked with chocolate chips. Savoring my treat, I rested my strained eyes and mentally prepared myself for the next stack. One set of graded compositions equated to several pounds of added weight. Tipping the scale at 170, I started doubting the integrity of my next best friend. Lethargic from weight gain and unmotivated to exercise, I defeatedly watched my waist expand, my thighs thicken, and my buttocks broaden. It wasn't a pretty sight.

ALL THINGS ARE POSSIBLE!

One Monday night in early April I habitually prepared myself for yet another paper grading marathon. Tapestry bag in one hand and peanut butter jar in the other, I headed towards the bedroom to commence my arduous task when suddenly an urge to go to church overwhelmed me. I intellectualized, "We don't have church services on Monday evenings," and I continued traipsing toward the bedroom. The urge persisted, but I rebuked it and started paper grading. Thirty minutes later, unable to concentrate on my compositions, I finally submitted, dressed, and drove to church. To my surprise the parking lot overflowed with vehicles. *I wonder what's going on*, I thought as I walked to the entrance. Approaching the sanctuary, I noticed a middle-aged man bubbling with excitement as he told his story.

"With God all things are possible. I'm living proof. I should be dead. Instead, I'm very much alive, and my heart muscle is stronger now than before my heart attack!" he shared.

He proceeded to tell of the coronary condition that destroyed the majority of his heart muscle. Doctors lost hope and sent him home to die. He and his wife, strong believers in God and the power of prayer, decided to pray for a miracle healing. This fellow believer now stood before the assembled congregation to testify to answered prayer.

The audience sat transfixed as the man, through many tears, relayed details of his story. Midway through his testimony, the man's wife stood, approached the podium, apologized to her husband for interrupting him and began:

"God revealed to me that there are individuals here who have been raped, molested, and sexually abused. You can receive healing from these past memories if you come to the altar for prayer."

Deafened to my surroundings, I riveted my eyes upon the speaker and waited for her to finish. As she concluded,

I immediately sprang from the pew, edged towards the aisle, and darted to the front of the church. My hasty advance admitted to the assembly my need and desire to receive what she offered. I determined not to leave church without it!

Desperate and hopeful, I knelt before the altar and waited to hear the magic word that would set me free from the past. Ministering to other individuals first, the speaker finally approached, placed her hand on my shoulder, and asked for a succinct description of the experience that brought me to the altar. I told her of the rape, the subsequent nightmares, and the relational dysfunction with men. With a discerning ear she astutely listened, lowered her head briefly as if in prayer, and then responded. "The answer to your emotional healing, Marlane, lies in forgiveness. You must forgive the man who raped you. What happened that night had nothing to do with sex. It had everything to do with power and control. That individual, probably feeling powerless and out of control in his own life, saw in you an opportunity to regain what he lacked. You must pray for him, wherever he is now in the world, and forgive him. Only then will God set you free from your emotional bondage."

What the woman shared made no logical sense to me at all. *Why should I forgive someone for hurting me so badly? He doesn't deserve forgiveness,* I internally reasoned. As if reading my thoughts, the woman continued:

"God commands us to forgive one another, no matter what the sin. All sin deserves forgiveness. The Bible says, 'If you want God to forgive you of your sins, you must forgive others their sins'" (Matthew 6:14).

I wrestled with her message. As a child of God I was to reflect God's love to the world in which I lived. That included forgiving others, regardless of their offenses. My pride warred with my spirit. Minutes later, the inner struggle ceased as I lowered my defenses, and with her guidance, prayed a prayer of forgiveness for the rapist.

"Please forgive my rapist for what he did to me," I whimpered, "and please forgive me for hating him all of these years." Tears began to roll down my cheeks. Although just a trickle at first, they increased with each spirit-cleansing word. I opened the floodgates of my emotional dam and released 17 years of pent-up anger, bitterness, and unforgiveness. My spiritual counselor held me tightly as I wailed. Haltingly, I prayed until my purged heart quieted. Silent, we reverently and peacefully remained at the foot of the altar. Imperceptibly my heart was transformed in that brief moment.

Minutes later, the counselor thanked God for what had just transpired and concluded our time together with a contemplative "Amen." I rose from my knees and gratefully embraced my new friend. Feeling freer than I had in the last 17 years, I returned to my pew.

Thus commenced the emotional healing process in my life. No, the elephant didn't completely vacate my living room that fortuitous night. I didn't hear bells or sirens, and my phobia towards men didn't magically disappear. Something notable did occur: the realistic nightmare of the rape, which nightly awakened me, ceased. When I looked at myself in the mirror, I could see a flicker of hope for the first time in many years. Newfound motivation to tackle and conquer my weight problem spurred me to don running clothes and pound a mile of pavement rather than dip into the peanut butter jar. Within months the scale sighed relief as my weight declined. Clothes, relegated to the back of my closet, reemerged, and for once I looked forward to dressing for work.

Teachers silently noted my weight loss; students verbalized it: "Hey, Miss Zillmann, you're looking great! Keep it up!" Encouraged by student cheerleaders, I gradually reformed my eating habits. Three balanced meals a day replaced the unhealthy practice of starving myself for breakfast and lunch and then gorging at dinner. Substituting fresh fruit and yogurt for peanut butter and chocolate chips, I still rewarded myself during the paper grading marathons, but not to the detriment of my figure or self-esteem. Slowly, one pound at a time, I returned to my desired weight.

The night I forgave the rapist, I started a weight-loss program. My heavy heart lightened, and through the on-going healing process, I gradually shed the cumbersome, heavy burdens of harbored bitterness, anger, and unfor-giveness. In time, Phil stopped calling me by my nick-name, and Hoover once again referred to the name of a vacuum cleaner!

CHAPTER 7

IS HE THE RIGHT ONE?

A dichotomy still existed in my heart when it came to men. On the one hand, I liked them, but on the other hand, I feared them. The emotional elephant of distrust in men had grown as I had gotten older.

"Always the bridesmaid, never the bride," I heard referred to me more than once at the many weddings of friends I attended throughout my 20s.

"Well, Marlane, when are you going to get married?" was a question I was asked all too often.

Outwardly smiling, I usually rattled off some flip comment such as, "I'm too busy with teaching and my other activities to think about getting serious with anyone right now." Inwardly crying, my wounded heart enviously screamed, "I want to get married. I'm lonely! I want someone special in my life, too! What's wrong with me?" Too fearful of the possible answer to this question, I subconsciously chose to ignore it. Thus, the revolving-door relationship pattern continued.

Men entered and exited my life throughout my 20s and early 30s, some more rapidly than others. I dismissed beaus my age as too immature for me and gravitated towards men at least ten years my senior. Since I dated multiple men concurrently, I was forced to book my social calendar months ahead. Dinner dates three or four times a week conveniently nourished me, and on the few nights I ate home alone, I sumptuously feasted on doggie bag leftovers. Occasionally, due to an exceptionally heavy dating week, the doggie bags accumulated and spoiled before I consumed them. Looking for yet another way to tease their only sister, my three brothers used my refrigerator and its prolific penicillin production ability as the butt for many a joke and ribbing.

"Under all of the fuzz, that distinctly looks like shrimp," Phil once quipped.

Each sibling, in turn, offered uproariously clever guesses as to the true identity of my refrigerator leftovers that were fully ensconced in mold. Phil went even a step further in his jibes.

"You're the only person I know," he observed, "who dusts her stove!" Crazy as it sounds, it was true. My male companions wined and dined me so lavishly that I rarely cooked or even grocery shopped.

Life was fun now that I had experienced the spiritual breakthrough in forgiving my rapist. On occasion several of my married teaching peers, listening to my adventures, said they secretly wished for the same freedom and opportunities I experienced. Unbeknownst to them, I envied their opportunity to go home at night and fall into the arms of one committed, loving man. In some ways their lives were less complicated than mine. After all, I had to keep the names of the various men straight in my mind so

I didn't inadvertently call someone by someone else's name. My married friends just had to remember the name of their spouse! Guilty of this faux pas occasionally, I'd sheepishly apologize to my "misnamed" male friend, when all the while I'm sure he wondered, *Who is that other guy anyway?*

Carefully checking my social calendar, I generally avoided awkward situations with my many male companions except for one inauspicious day. What was I thinking? I deliberately scheduled two dates with two different men on the same day. The first commitment supposedly lasted from morning to mid-afternoon. *No problem,* I reasoned. *I'll have plenty of time to change and prepare for my evening date. I can do this.* Famous last words.

The day of infamy began peacefully and progressed smoothly until afternoon. Unforeseen circumstances arose, though, delaying our return as scheduled. Unassumingly glancing at my watch and noting the time, I felt my heartbeats quicken and my blood pressure rise. My date, relishing his precious time with me and oblivious to the impending conflict, merrily drove the posted speed limit. *Why, of all days, couldn't he break the speed limit, even a little?* I selfishly thought as I squirmed within. Nearing my home, I again checked the time. *Whew! Fifteen minutes to spare! I'll discreetly say good-bye to one, quickly change clothes, and calmly await the arrival of the next. I still can do this.*

Accelerating to the crest of my street, Date #1 exclaimed: "Marlane, there's a car in your driveway. Are you expecting someone?" A hot flash of embarrassment choked me.

"Funny you should ask. There's someone I'd like you

to meet." We pulled into the driveway just as date #2, unsuccessfully reaching me at the house, returned to his car. Recognizing me in the front seat with another man, he quizzically grimaced. *Here we go.* I dreaded the next seemingly eternal 30 seconds. "Tim, this is Joe; Joe, this is Tim."

I have no idea what they discussed after that brief introduction. Speaking not another word, I guiltily slithered into the house and prepared for my next date. All I know is that when I emerged from my home minutes later, adorned in evening attire, only one car occupied my driveway. Neither Date #2 nor I mentioned the incident again, and after a few moments of awkwardness, I was able to fully focus on the present and make small talk while silently repeating Date #2's name. This wasn't the time for yet another faux pas!

UNCONDITIONAL LOVE

This thrilling, adventuresome lifestyle complicated with time. From my naive perspective I saw no conflicts whatsoever. I harbored no hidden agenda. I sincerely enjoyed the fellowship and friendship of each male friend. Period. Viewing my chronological peers as brothers and my older beaus as father figures, I felt safe and secure with those familiar, pure male role models I experienced as a child. Needless to say, my male friends' agendas differed significantly from mine. Each investment of time, energy, and money represented one further step towards wooing me, winning me, and marrying me. Five of them, venturing into the forbidden zone beyond a platonic relationship, intrepidly strove for commitment and intimacy, much to their peril and our relational demise! Though he never got the ring, one unwavering warrior withstood the Dr.

Jekyll/Mr. Hyde wrath of Marlane, demonstrated the meaning of unconditional love, and helped prepare me for marriage. That brave individual was Les.

We met at a church Christian singles' event, a place I deemed safe to make male acquaintances. A strong, yet gentle, godly man, Les treated me like a queen. Consequently I felt safe and secure in his company. Months of seeing one another melted into years, and content though I was with the dating situation, Les grew impatient. One night, following an absolutely delightful dinner and concert, Les walked me to my side door and asked whether he could come in for a minute to talk.

"Sure," I casually responded. "I don't have to get up early tomorrow morning."

Sitting in the dimly lit living room, Les reached for my hand. "Marlane, we've dated each other several years now and have experienced many wonderful things together." I nodded in agreement. "The more time I've spent with you the more time I want to be with you." I again nodded, totally unaware of where the conversation was headed. Grasping for the right words, Les finally confessed: "What I'm trying to say is, I love you. I want to marry you." I mechanically started to nod again when the reality of his words pierced my intellect.

"You want to what?" I shrieked in disbelief.

"I want to marry you," Les reiterated.

I lost it. Flying into a verbal rage, I screamed: "I can't handle this! You weren't supposed to get serious with me. This ruins everything!"

Les sat, paralyzed by my unfamiliar behavior. Minutes later he rose and left the house in silence. I didn't hear from him for days.

In the meantime I contacted my parents and matter-of-factly informed them of my marriage proposal. "Should I marry him, Mom and Dad? Is he the right one?"

"If you have to ask us," Mom responded, "then he's not the right person."

That settled that. I knew what I'd tell Les if I ever talked to him again. After the way I verbally treated him, I understood if he wanted to sever the relationship completely without further discussion.

Three days later I received a call. "Marlane, this is Les. We need to talk. May I come over?"

Guilt-ridden and repentant, I sheepishly replied, "Okay."

Palms sweating and heart pounding, I awaited the arrival of his elegant silver Cadillac. As his incoming headlights bathed the kitchen floor, I emotionally braced myself, uttered a brief prayer, and meekly unlocked the door to greet my soon-to-be former boy friend. A miraculous conversation ensued.

Unable to make eye contact, I ashamedly muttered, "I'm so sorry, Les, for the terrible way I treated you."

Not a word did he speak for several minutes. Then he gently raised my crestfallen chin and lovingly looked me in the eye. "Last Friday night I didn't know what to think when I drove away from your house. I'd never seen this side of you before. To be honest, it scared me. I spent a lot of time seeking God in prayer. I wanted to make some sense of what happened. After much soul searching, I believe God showed me what's going on inside of you. Based on your past traumatic rape experience, you fear intimacy and commitment. Therefore, unknowingly, you've insulated yourself from romantic, emotional feelings and consciously control every relationship to avoid any surprises you might not be able to handle. Everything went well until, unknowingly, I crossed that unspoken line and posed a potential threat to your safety and security. Defending yourself through your vicious outburst of rage, you intended merely to protect yourself. The Father showed me there's a spiritual battle waging within your soul. That meanness and wickedness aren't the real you.

"God wants you to experience His unconditional love that will never hurt you or disappoint you. He instructed me to stand firm and shower you with unconditional love regardless of how you treat me. Marlane, no matter how difficult you make life, I promise I'll love you with God's love."

Les kept his promise. Our friendship continued, and at times when my emotional elephant reared its ugly head and I instinctively lashed out in anger, his commitment to love me unconditionally was tested. Dependable, honest, and trustworthy, he stood on the rock of his faith and in turn remained faithful to me. Though never to become my husband, Les played an instrumental part in teaching me the true meaning of unconditional love.

CHAPTER 8

MT. ST. HELENS—WATCH OUT!

T he violent, ugly outbursts to which Les referred had plagued me so long I felt they would always be a part of me. "You always hurt the ones you love the most." This proved true in my life, especially concerning my mother. I remained a dormant, emotional volcano as long as life proceeded peacefully—i.e., no one lied to me, no one tried to control me, and no one offered me constructive criticism. My fragile, negative self-esteem cloaked itself in an air of superiority that I unconsciously used as a defense mechanism to prevent acquaintances from getting too close and thus discovering the real me. My mom knew the real me—the good, the bad, and the ugly. As a concerned, loving parent responsible for disciplining her daughter, Mom often stirred up my hidden rage in her effort to confront the sins of my life and help me grow.

One day, walking into the kitchen, she interrupted me in the middle of my snack (this was during my years of uncontrolled eating). Knife in hand, I generously smeared peanut butter on top of sandwich cookies and mechanically gobbled them. By the time she entered the kitchen, I'd already devoured at least a dozen.

Observing my obsessive behavior and desiring to help me recognize and stop this self-destructive act, she calmly asked, "Marlane, are you sure you want to pig out on those sandwich cookies and peanut butter?"

Without realizing it, she had pushed my control button. Instinctively, the quiet volcano erupted and defensively spewed angry words at my innocent mother as I snapped back,

"Don't tell me what I should and shouldn't do. I'll eat whatever I feel like eating!" Then I proceeded to voraciously eat an additional dozen cookies, just to spite her.

Mom didn't deserve this kind of response, and I knew it. Surprised and embarrassed by my irrational reaction to such a benign situation, I apologized for my thoughtless, mean comments and display of disrespect, all the while promising it would never happen again. But happen it did, again and again and again.

When I was a teenager, my mom chalked it up to hormones, but as this behavior persisted past college and into adult life, she mustered up her courage and confronted me one day.

She quietly said, "I'm concerned about you. There's an anger within, over which you have no control. You need counseling so you can resolve it."

"What do you mean?" I erupted once again. "I don't have a problem with anger!" I bellowed, storming out of the room.

I didn't want to hear the truth. I couldn't handle the truth. My facade of perfectionism had fooled the general public into believing I had my act together. Acquaintances, duped by my convincing acting job, felt intimidated by my impeccable behavior. Comparing their flaws and humanness to what they saw in me, they felt inferior and consequently refrained from establishing close relationships. *I could never be as good as Marlane,* they inaccurately concluded. If they only knew. Terrified of exposing the real me to the wrong people, I zealously guarded my emotions and openly revealed them only to a very small list of safe people: Mom, Bruce (my teaching friend), and Dan (my future husband), because they loved and accepted me no matter how I behaved. Each dealt with my inappropriate outbursts of anger in his or her own way. Mom confronted me with them, and Bruce tried to overlook them. Dan, constantly walking on eggshells, qualified everything he said so as not to ignite my ire, which having once witnessed, he constantly feared.

I couldn't risk counseling; counseling would announce to the world I had a problem, and I couldn't handle that. "Not on your life will I go to counseling. Never!" I vehemently proclaimed as I slammed my bedroom door in protest. *How dare she try to tell me what to do. I'm an adult now and can take care of myself. Thank you, but no thank you!*

Fear and pride consumed me. I intellectually knew what the Bible said about anger: "Be angry, but do not sin" (Ephesians 4:26). Somehow, though, I misinterpreted it to mean: "Good Christian girls don't get angry." I couldn't acknowledge my sin of anger if I wanted to be a good Christian girl, I reasoned. Secretly fearing what I'd discover if I ever acknowledged my anger and delved into the precipitating factors behind it, I chose instead to deny it. The person who tried so hard to model an exemplary godly life was no more than a hypocrite and a liar. Although I fooled a lot of unsuspecting people, I didn't fool my heavenly Father. I detested living in my angry skin, but I felt trapped. The path to emotional freedom lay in simple humility, honesty, confrontation, and confession, but I feared facing the truth of my life. So I continued burying my head in the sand and ignoring the elephant all while the volcano smoldered.

CHAPTER 9

YOUR AD DIDN'T LIE

I never seriously considered marriage during the first 34 years of my life. After all, I already was married to teaching. Unaware of my relational weaknesses due to the elephant, I blamed my singleness on time constraints due to my teaching commitment. Despite the fact that most teachers found time to marry and have families, I thought this impossible in my case. I thought that I couldn't successfully minister to my students and still have time to nurture a quality relationship with a husband and possibly children.

Incessantly pestered by well-meaning family and friends about my marriage intentions, I started feeling self-conscious about my singleness and periodically asked myself, *What's wrong with me that I'm not married?* In search of an answer to this question, I flew to California for a singles' conference and heard a keynote speaker utter a wise principle that put to rest my increasing feelings of desperation: "It's better to be happily single than unhappily married." Returning to Cleveland, I vowed to live a fulfilled, happy single life and not spend my energy and time worrying about the possibility of marriage. That day an emotional weight fell off my shoulders as I conclusively placed my expectations of marriage into God's hands and announced to family and friends, "If God wants me to marry, He'll put that desire in my heart when He knows the timing is right."

For almost three years, while casually dating several wonderful men, I cultivated an ever closer relationship with the Lord. This precious, intimate time with Him prepared me for January 1987.

GOD'S TIMING AT LAST

When I least expected it, God changed my heart. Awakening one fortuitous, snowy Sunday morning, for the first time in my life I experienced an overwhelming desire to share the good and bad of life with someone special. After 34 years of singleness I felt it was now God's perfect timing to show me the one He'd chosen for me.

Eating lunch after church that day, I told my parents about this sudden change of heart. My mother lightheartedly suggested, "God's got a great sense of humor. Why don't you put a personal ad in *The Cleveland Magazine* and see if He uses that means to introduce you to your husband?"

"You've got to be kidding! Tell me you're joking."

"I couldn't be more serious. What do you have to lose?"

Kurt, my youngest brother, chimed in. "I'll even help you write the ad. We'll make it a group effort. Let's have some fun!" Despite continued mild protestations and utter disbelief that my mom could even think of such a way to help find God's choice of a spouse for me, I conceded, and by afternoon's end my brother, mom, dad, and I authored the following ad:

"Thirty-four, attractive, professional, born-again lady, loves outdoors, theater, fine dining, swimming, sailing, never married, non-smoker, seeks life partner." Chuckling to myself as I mailed the ad and $104 fee, I thought, *I can't wait to see what's going to come of this!* Little did I know that was the best $104 I ever spent.

In my heart I started concocting a list of requirements for Mr. Right: handsome, educated, outdoorsy, humorous, athletic, and Christian. Never would I marry a divorced man, that was one thing for sure! Just five years before, a dear godly woman who was a second mother to me shared a dream she had regarding my future. She said I'd marry an older, previously married man, and I'd have children, though none from my womb. She encouraged me to tuck this vision away into the depths of my heart, which I did. I'd nearly forgotten it when I met Dan.

Dr. Daniel S. Renner, a respected cardiovascular thoracic surgeon on the east side of Cleveland, opened the latest *Cleveland Magazine*. As a subscriber, he had the privilege of receiving his issue before it hit the newsstand. Curiosity gripped his heart when he read my ad. *This sounds too good to be true,* he thought, as he penned a brief note to the post office box number and slipped it into the mail.

The next week I received a manila envelope crammed with 21 letters from interested men. This overwhelming response pleased me greatly! Before I began poring over the correspondences, I prayed, "Show me which letters You want me to answer." He did. The following Tuesday I arranged a date with an engineer at a local Thai restaurant. The evening couldn't have been more delightful. He was a Christian, educated, athletic, and good looking. Previously married, he'd been recently divorced. Several days after our date, I received a touching letter from him. He told me I was everything and more than he'd ever expected or hoped to meet on a blind date. Realizing I was ready for marriage, he knew he still needed time to heal from his divorce. He thanked me for a most enjoyable evening and wished me God's best.

That next day, a day I'll never forget, I met Dan. We arranged to meet at a pizza restaurant. A neophyte when it came to blind dates, I chose a restaurant where I knew the proprietor and consequently felt safe. Dan and I told each other what we'd be wearing so we could identify each other from amongst the crowd. Nervously but excitedly, I prepared for this new adventure. Could this be the one?

Dan arrived 20 minutes late. The owner directed him towards my table, and before I could say a word of introduction he exclaimed, "Your ad didn't lie."

"What?"

"Your ad didn't lie. You said you were attractive, and you are." Thus began our nearly two-hour uninterrupted conversation. The numerous interests we shared included canoeing, hiking, biking, animals, gardening. It was unbelievable!

Could he be for real? I wondered.

Forthright and open from the outset, he inquired, "What's your feeling about having a family?"

"I love children, obviously, but I don't feel the need to have a child in order to be fulfilled as a woman," I explained.

"Well, you answered that correctly," he said.

"What do you mean?"

"I've worked hard for many years so I could have the opportunity to travel and be free. I really don't want to start another family at this time in my life." (At this time Dan was 54, twenty years my senior.)

The time flew by and our conversation unfolded naturally and comfortably. At nearly 7:00 p.m. Dan looked at his watch and exclaimed: "Wow, it's getting late. I need to be at a hospital dinner meeting at 7:30. Do you have to be anywhere special at any specific time?"

"In fact, I do. I promised one of my students I'd support him at his Eagle Court of Honor ceremony tonight at 7:30."

"You haven't had anything to eat, have you? Why don't I order you a meal. I'll be eating at the hospital in a half hour, but I might bum a little food from you to stave off my hunger." Thus our ritual of sharing meals began.

As the time neared 7:30, we bid each other adieu. Walking me to my car, Dan softly, innocently kissed my cheek and said, "I'll call you." Deep down inside I knew he would. I floated to the Boy Scout Court of Honor!

Twitterpated, as he later described his feelings, he drove to the hospital shaking his head and mumbling, *Can this be true? Is she for real?* That night he knew there was something different about me, and he liked what he saw.

I, too, knew there was something different about this man. Never had I felt this way about anyone before. Mom's sage words of old echoed in my memory: "When you meet the right person, you'll know."

"Sure," I had replied facetiously. Guess what, she was right! He turned me on intellectually as well as physically.

Due to our busy work and previously arranged dating

schedules, we parted company with no firm plans for a second date. God had His plan, though. A week later He sovereignly arranged for a major spring snowstorm that closed down Mayfield High School. At 5:30 that morning I arose to a deep blanket of snow outside and quickly dressed to shovel the driveway so I could get to work on time.

I charged into the house at nearly 7:00 a.m., sweaty, aching, and exhausted from the arduous shoveling job, only to find the answering machine incessantly blinking away. While slaving away outside, I had received two phone calls on my answering machine. The first, from my department chairman, told me to turn off my alarm, go back to bed, and enjoy the day.

Childlike elation thrilled me as I heard the familiar voice of my department head. "Yippee, I don't have to go to school!" I shouted.

I loved snow days, the only paid holidays for teachers. The thought quickly crossed my mind to have breakfast and then dive into my stack of ungraded papers; that is, until I heard the second message, which came from Dan:

"I heard Mayfield schools are closed for the day, so you have to be free. How about going cross country skiing with me after my office hours? Give me a call."

I loved cross country skiing, and the absolutely perfect weather conditions prompted me to reach for the phone and give Dan a call.

A Friendship Begins

What an exhilarating day we spent together! Arduously forging ski tracks through three feet of virgin snow, we took turns taking the lead and childishly playing little tricks on one another.

"Stand right here for a minute," Dan suggested.

"Why?"

"You'll see," he laughed as he violently shook the fir tree branch overhead and buried me up to my waist in fluffy white stuff.

"I'll get you!" I promised, dislodging myself from the snow drift. Totally bedecked in white and looking like none other than the abominable snowman, I zealously skied after him in swift pursuit and tackled him to the ground, giving him a small dose of his own medicine! Minutes turned into hours. We skied heartily and laughed even more heartily. How natural and at home with himself Dan appeared, and I felt the same way around him. He freely laughed at my puns and even created a few himself. By day's end we were mentally exhausted from punishing each other so much.

Thus began our friendship. Needless to say, I never contacted any of the 19 remaining possible beaus from my personal ad. By June, Dan decided to date me exclusively, and although I continued to see my other male friends on a casual basis, I knew deep down inside that Dan was Mr. Right.

Our friendship blossomed rapidly, much faster than I ever anticipated, and as Dan verbalized his romantic feelings towards me, Mr. Hyde didn't rear his ugly head even once as he had so often done in the past when presented with other men's advances. Somehow, this time, everything seemed different. A traditional romantic, I advised Dan that if he ever had intentions of marrying me, he'd have to first ask my father for my hand in marriage.

In early November of 1987, Dan invited me and my parents to attend the Playhouse Square performance of the musical "Cats." As Dan dropped my mother and me off at the entrance to the theater, he said, "Rudy, why don't you come with me to park the car?" Not until weeks later did I understand his motive.

On Thanksgiving Day, after a romantic, candlelit dinner, Dan popped the question. "What would you say if I asked you to marry me?"

Totally surprised and caught off guard, but, strangely enough, not feeling threatened, I said, "I need to pray about it. Give me some time."

After four torturous days of waiting for a reply, Dan received my answer: "Yes, I'll marry you."

Choking back grateful tears, he responded, "You've made me very happy."

And Two Became One

July 30, 1988, eight months later, I walked down the aisle adorned in an elegant, long-trained ivory wedding gown bedecked with sequins and pearls, the dress chosen by my father. Surrounded by more than 400 supportive guests, loving family, and 16 bridesmaids and groomsmen, Dan and I exchanged vows of eternal commitment to God and to one another.

In His perfect timing and with His great sense of humor, God sovereignly brought together two people—a doctor and a teacher—who unknowingly lived within a few miles of each other for years. We discovered that I had taught Dan's stepson English at Mayfield High School five years prior to our meeting, and that my gynecologist shared office space with Dan, so I most likely had crossed paths with him during annual doctor's appointments but never realized the significance of it.

The day I married Dr. Dan Renner, an older man with four grown children and two grandchildren, I fulfilled the vision God gave my friend five years before.

CHAPTER 10

A LIFETIME OF ADVENTURE

"I'm looking forward to a lifetime of adventure with you, Marlane," Dan pledged at the wedding altar that steamy July afternoon, and less than eight hours later he started fulfilling that commitment.

An action-packed candlelight dinner/dance reception followed and was attended by relatives, teacher friends, doctors, and 40 of my favorite students at one of downtown Cleveland's most elegant facilities. Afterwards, Dan and I, emotionally and physically exhausted, were driven to our hotel to enjoy our long-awaited, much-anticipated romantic honeymoon getaway. My brother Phil and his family, dropping us off at the hotel in the wee hours of the morning, thoroughly expected we'd cozily settle into our pre-paid honeymoon suite long before they arrived home, but plans changed.

Dressed in our wedding garb and laden with suitcases, we approached the registration desk, and Dan drowsily yet proudly announced, "Dr. and Mrs. Daniel Renner to check into the honeymoon suite."

"Just a minute, Dr. Renner," replied the hotel clerk. Awaiting our room key, we casually conversed with another bridal couple anxiously looking forward to their special night as well. Seconds turned into minutes as two tired souls yearned for their key to rest.

"Sorry for the delay, sir. We don't know what happened, but somehow we've given away your room. I'm sorry." Instantaneously, and to the surprise and relief of the manager, both Dan and I broke into uncontrolled laughter.

"Our lifetime of adventure has begun!" Dan exclaimed as I nodded in agreement.

"We can give you a regular room and then offer you a complimentary pass to the hospitality suite so you can enjoy a continental breakfast in the morning," the hotel manager proffered.

"That won't be satisfactory, sir," Dan calmly, yet firmly, explained. "We've paid for the honeymoon suite and have already arranged a breakfast cruise on the Cuyahoga River for 118 of our wedding guests later this morning."

"Let me see what else we can do, Dr. Renner," said the manager as he retreated to the back room. Minutes later he emerged with a generous, more-feasible suggestion. "I've already called a cab to pick you up and take you to the Bond Court Hotel down the street. Due to the inconvenience we've caused you on your special night, we'll be more than happy to pay for your accommodations. Please accept our full apology." Dan, glancing at me and looking for a nod of approval, saw the sparkle of excitement in my eye and immediately accepted the hotel manager's offer.

Picking up our luggage, we headed for the hotel's front door and our awaiting cab, but not before we extended a sincere good luck to the weary bridal couple next in line.

Blaring horns of congratulation destroyed the early morning silence. "Way to go," taxi drivers yelled into the cool, refreshing early morning air as they sped past our open-window vehicle. Too tired to respond, we just gratefully smiled at our well-wishers.

Finally at 1:30 a.m., bleary-eyed, we crossed the threshold of our newly arranged bridal suite, a spacious accommodation complete with living room, kitchen, and bathroom larger than most people's bedrooms. Needless to say, it exceeded our wildest expectations! "Now this is what I call an adventure!" Dan beamed, voraciously munching down a room-service hamburger and fries with his new bride at his side.

After a short but restful sleep in our castle, we checked out and joined our 118 wedding guests dockside for the breakfast river cruise, excitedly sharing with them the story of the first of what would be many adventures of our married life. Dan truly was a man of his word!

CHAPTER 11

LEAVE AND CLEAVE

"**F**or this cause a man shall leave his father and mother and shall cleave to his wife" (Gen. 2:24).

God knew that failure to break strong, dependent parental ties before entering marriage would lead to deep problems in the marital relationship. That's why He wisely mentioned this paramount principle at the very beginning of the Bible. Though the minister seriously stated this point during our wedding vows, I only half heard it, but didn't heed it until our month-old marriage started to flounder, and I desperately searched for the reason.

The first 35 years of my life I remained single, emotionally married to God and, unknowingly, to my parents. The closest bonds I had with anyone on this earth existed with my mom and dad. Holding them in high esteem and placing them on a pedestal, I denied the truth that they were human just like everyone else. Whatever they said I took as gospel, and as I grew up, I unconsciously adopted many of their political and personal beliefs and opinions. While a teenager, I remember asking my mom's advice on various topics of concern. When she told me her views, I automatically took them as my own without spending time to ponder just how I felt about them. I reasoned, *It's easier that way. After all, she's so much older and wiser. Why waste time analyzing and processing data concerning the certain situation, only to come up with the same solution in the end?* Without realizing it, I fell into this bad habit. Easy, yes; healthy, no. With no personal thoughts or opinions, I robotically responded as if I were a clone of my parents. This behavior continued for years until I neared high school graduation. Then came a day that changed my life forever.

On this particular afternoon I recall asking my mom's opinion on a certain topic. I automatically expected to receive her wise answer, but no such thing happened. Instead, for the first time I ever remember, my mom asked, "Well, what do you think?"

Stunned, I repeated my initial question. Maybe she didn't hear me. Again she replied, "What do you think?"

I didn't like that response one bit and let her know. No matter how I tried to rephrase my question, she responded in like fashion. I felt betrayed and rejected.

"Don't you love me? Don't you care about me?" I asked dejectedly.

"That's the problem. I do love you, and I do care about you," she replied. "I care about you so much I realize you need to start thinking for yourself so you can stand on your own two feet. When you go off to college, we won't be around to help you make decisions. Time is short, and you have a lot to learn. The truth is, I love you so much that I won't tell you how I feel about something anymore until you take time to analyze the situation and come up with a solution on your own."

The tears welled up in my eyes as Mom hugged me and tried to reassure me of her love. On the outside I acted hurt and rejected, but deep inside I knew she was right. I was scared.

Throughout the rest of my senior year she stuck to her guns in this matter, and, consequently, I sailed through college making my own decisions for the most part. I called home for advice rarely, and the postal service handled most of the correspondence between my folks and me. I slowly matured.

OLD HABITS DIE HARD

Following college, I returned to Cleveland and began my teaching career. A neophyte, I experienced the normal fears and insecurities of any first-year teacher. So what did I do? I called Mom and Dad, of course. Fortunately (or possibly unfortunately, as the case may be), they came to the rescue and ministered to my emotional needs. Unknowingly, I started deferring to their opinions and suggestions once again. The adult/child relationship re-emerged, and their twenty-one-year-old daughter relapsed once more into emotional dependency.

The first five years of teaching were filled with anxiety and stress, which promoted this dependency. Without a boyfriend per se and an unusual living situation (renting rooms in people's homes and sharing apartments), my parents became my major sounding board for thoughts and decisions as well as my means of escape. Friday afternoons at 3:30, following a tiring week at school, I ran to my already-packed car and raced home to Bay Village (before rush hour began) for some much-needed physical and emotional rest. What started as an occasional visit during my first month of teaching soon became my regular practice. Even if I dated on a Friday evening, I headed for the west side late that same night or early the next morning to spend the remainder of the weekend with my parents. I resumed church attendance there, which further obligated me to perpetuate the close ties with my folks.

I loved the arrangement, for it seemed to meet all of my needs—emotional and physical—and my parents liked it because they enjoyed the close fellowship they so missed when I attended college. At the same time they realized that at my age I should have been seeking more independence, not dependence.

One day Mom broached the subject: "Why not stay over on your side of town every once in a while? Your father and I love your company, but don't you think you should make friends with people your own age in your own neighborhood? We're not always going to be around, you know."

I didn't want to hear that. Deep down inside I knew she was right, but fear again surfaced. *What if I reached out to befriend people and they rejected me? Why risk it?* I felt safe in the current arrangement. With all the turmoil connected with teaching, coaching, and attending graduate school, I needed one constant source of peace in my life, and I found it in my weekly Bay Village retreat with my loving parents. So I resisted a change in lifestyle. Mom and Dad, sensing my insecurities, dropped the subject.

THE PROBLEMS BEGAN

For the previous 34 years I'd shared every intimate detail of my life with my mother. I kept no secrets, nor could I. She knew me so well she read my mind. One look into my eyes and she knew what I thought or felt. This transparency was all well and good, to a point. When I continued to feel obligated to unravel every detail of my life to my confessor after meeting Dan, the problems began.

After Dan entered my life, our relationship progressed rapidly. Although I owned my own home on the east side and didn't commute weekly to Bay Village, I still maintained a strong emotional attachment with my parents, especially my mom. Dan had noticed it immediately and asked me, "Do you tell your parents everything you do?"

When I replied, "Almost everything," a red flag raised in his mind.

Am I marrying an emotional child in a 35-year-old body? he thought but never verbalized until years later. So our relationship continued, and I remained unaware that a potential problem existed.

After we exchanged wedding vows, the honeymoon continued for a month until the first major crisis occurred. Instinctively I called home to cry on my parents' shoulders instead of going directly to my husband to resolve the conflict. (After all, as their daughter, they'd most likely side with me in the matter.) Had I done this only occasionally, there would have been no reason for concern. Unfortunately, this behavior continued. I started dragging Mom and Dad into the middle of our conflicts, and Dan didn't like that one bit.

"They have no business knowing everything that goes on behind closed doors!" he ranted one day after he found out I'd spilled all of the beans to my folks.

Angrily, I shot back, "I can tell them anything I want about our married life. After all, they're my parents!"

Realizing we'd reached a stalemate, Dan conceded, but secretly decided he could no longer confide in his bride.

This decision both hurt and angered him. He displayed his anger over the situation in subtle ways. His interaction with my folks changed dramatically. Previously very patient with them, now the slightest character defect on their part agitated him. Noticing his impatience and erratic temper swings when my parents visited, I jumped all over Dan in their defense.

"You don't show my parents the love and respect they deserve!" I criticized. "That hurts me. Don't you know they're the most important people in my whole life?"

This cut Dan to the quick and understandably so. The day we exchanged wedding vows, Dan rightfully should have become the most important human being in my life, yet I had just confessed he took a distant third to my parents. Violating God's principle of "leaving one's parents and cleaving to the spouse," I unintentionally pitted Dan against my folks, which created an intense jealousy and subsequent power play. This, in turn, drove a deeper wedge of anger and bitterness between him and me. Though I refused to admit it, I was to blame.

CHAPTER 12

THE FALL GUY

M y precious, loving husband became the fall guy for
the problems in our marriage, whether he deserved
it or not. I was afraid to admit my mistakes or see
the elephant so large and overpowering right in my living
room. Unwilling to accept personal responsibility for my
inappropriate actions, I perched on top of my sanctimo-
nious pedestal of perfection and judgmentally pointed the
finger of blame towards anyone or anything but me. Quick
to judge others who sinned, I rebelled against constructive
criticism aimed at me and zealously defended my actions
so as to justify them to others (and myself). To the unsuspecting world, I appeared self-confident and secure; un-
derneath the facade, I didn't know who Marlane really
was. Years of denying my true emotions and stuffing them
deep inside eventually took its toll.

Up to this point, I'd never fully addressed the elephant
in my living room and the subsequent control and honesty

70

issues which caused me to violently spew my anger onto all whom I loved, especially my dear husband, who had now become the closest male, both physically and emotionally, to me. Therefore, on many occasions he undeservedly received much of my deferred rage. Each time Dan unknowingly pushed an emotional button of unresolved hurt from my past, I instinctively reacted with all of the pent-up anger harbored towards Herb, the rapist, rather than responding appropriately to the issue at hand with my husband.

The issues weren't necessarily earth shattering either. Any way in which I felt Dan tried to control me and force his wishes on me caused my dander to rise. Early in the marriage, for example, World War III almost broke out when we dealt with the major marital issue of which position to leave the toilet seat in after use—up or down. I adamantly insisted that Dan lower it after use. He blatantly refused my demand. Wasting needless hours arguing over this ridiculous issue, I wouldn't waver from my stubborn opinion.

"What makes you think you're right?" Dan questioned.

"I'm obviously correct. No one in his right mind leaves a toilet seat up after use. It's not refined."

The real issue had nothing to do with right or wrong; it had everything to do with control. I could have cared less about what was proper or improper. Under no circumstance would I allow Dan to control me. After all, twenty-six years ago I let another guy control me, and I never forgot what happened. Never again!

MASK OF SUPERIORITY

I always had to be right any time we discussed anything of substance, especially controversial issues like abortion. My unspoken goal of any conversation was to conform Dan to my opinion on the subject. If he refused to see things my way, I goaded him until he relinquished and verbally agreed with me, even though, deep down, he steadfastly held to his own convictions. Not until later in our marriage did I realize how much I had tried to control him. A mask of superiority blinded me from recognizing my real feelings of inferiority.

In my eyes, every discussion had to have a winner and a loser; I couldn't agree to disagree. Dan—an intelligent, free-thinking individual—rebelled. Mature and emotionally controlled, he walked away from the brewing arguments in an effort to diffuse the emotions before they got out of control. On the other hand, I refused to give up the fight until I claimed victory, so what did I do? I followed Dan to the bedroom, or wherever he retreated, to continue the discussion. (I didn't want to let the enemy get away without a fight!)

"I won't argue with you," he sternly proclaimed as he turned heel and withdrew once again to avoid a scene. Persistently and obnoxiously argumentative, I one day pushed him so far that he ran to the darkroom and locked himself inside to avoid the imminent battle and my irrational wrath. After minutes of pounding on the door and shouting at him to no avail, I realized if I wanted to fight, I'd have to fight alone. Dan wasn't going to give me the satisfaction of fighting with him; he stalwartly refused to sink to my immature level of behavior. Lowering my fists and bridling my tongue, I finally surrendered that battle, but deep inside my soul the war still raged and the power struggle continued.

Life returned to some semblance of normalcy for a brief period of time until another button push thrust me into the next battle. This sick behavior continued until the day I hit rock bottom.

CHAPTER 13

ROCK BOTTOM

I n August 1993, the minister of our church asked me to co-chair the women's ministry for the June 1994 Cleveland Billy Graham Crusade. This responsibility required attendance at all crusade planning committee meetings and accountability to the church women for the upcoming events of the crusade.

Heavily involved in community volunteer efforts, especially the local hospital auxiliary, I had virtually no free time and already felt overcommitted to the point of sacrificing my peace and joy in an effort to serve the Lord. The day the pastor phoned me, I perfunctorily informed him, "I'll have to pray about it and talk to Dan. Then I'll get back to you." Hanging up the phone, I felt a sudden, overwhelming fire of anticipation and excitement ignite within my heart, although at the time I couldn't discern its deeper significance.

"Well, how do you feel about it?" Dan asked me. "Is it something you'd like to do?"

"I'd love it," I replied. "How do you feel about me doing it? It's going to require a lot of my time, and there will be quite a few evenings when I won't be able to be at home with you. Is that okay?"

"Certainly. If you'd like to take on the challenge, I'm behind you 100% of the way."

"Thanks, sweetheart. I'll give the pastor a call to-morrow."

CHANCE OF A LIFETIME

The thought of fellowshiping and praying with other children of God throughout the city thrilled me! *I have to make sure I provide quality time in my schedule to undertake these responsibilities,* I reasoned. Thus, I began revising my schedule to accommodate this additional undertaking. I knew the opportunity was a once-in-a-lifetime chance since the aging Billy Graham might never return to Cleveland. I finally decided to place this commitment at the top of my priority list for the coming year. Resigning or taking a hiatus from all sorts of positions and organizations, I made a concerted effort to devote quality time to this new endeavor. God had other intentions for the new-found free time in my life, though.

Planning meetings began in September. Monthly get-togethers gave way to bi-weekly meetings as the time neared for the crusade. During the fall months, after I cleared my schedule but had not yet jumped fully into the crusade preparations, I started to do something I hadn't done in many years—think about a lot of things. With free time on my hands (a novel experience for me), I allowed my mind to wander from one subject to another and one emotion to another. It felt strange and uncomfortable. For the last 20 years, I was so busy going to school, working, and volunteering that I never took time to slow down and get in touch with my feelings. (In reality, I probably subconsciously feared doing so because of the possible intense pain it would cause.) Now I had the time to think, and the more I thought, I realized how unhappy I was beneath the surface veneer of contentment. As I examined my life each passing day, I sank frighteningly deeper and deeper into depression, and misery consumed me.

In October, our church choir performed a musical, entitled "God With Us," and I cried through much of the performances. Only by God's strength and grace did I sing and not break down completely. I sobbed through two songs as the words convicted my heart:

Be strong and take courage. Do not fear or be dismayed; For the Lord will go before you, and His light will show the way. Be strong and take courage. Do not fear or be dismayed; For the One who lives within you will be strong in you today. Why don't you give Him all of your fears? Why don't you let Him wipe all of your tears? He knows! He's been thru pain before, and He knows all that you've been looking for. So be strong and take courage, do not fear or be dismayed; For the Lord will go before you, and His light will show the way. Nothing can take you out of His hand; Nothing can face you that He can't command. I know that you will always be in His love; In His power you will be free.

At this time of my life I felt emotionally imprisoned with no hope of escape. Bound. Afraid. Yet God reminded me through this song that all was not lost. There was a way to escape this prison—through Him. I could be free if I released my fears to Him and, in faith, entrusted my future to Him to guide and direct my life. Victory was possible, but I had to want it badly enough to surrender to Him.

The next song pierced my soul as well:

God will make a way where there seems to be no way. He works in ways we cannot see. He will make a way for me. He will be my guide, hold me closely to His side. With love and strength for each new day, He will make a way, God will make a way. He will do something new today.

In my increasing despair I allowed Satan to rob me of the hope found in the heavenly Father. As my life blackened with each passing day, my eyes blinded to His promise, "With God all things are possible" (Matthew 19:26). Instead of greeting each new morning with an attitude of gratitude and eagerly anticipating the day's exciting events, I dreaded waking up, lacked motivation to do much of anything, isolated myself from others, and couldn't wait to go to bed again. Not living, but merely existing, I resigned myself into believing I'd passed the point of no return. With no visible way out of the emotional hole into which I'd dug myself, I truly hit rock bottom.

CHAPTER 14
MISSION IMPOSSIBLE

od knew what it would take to get my attention.
Pride, my major stumbling block, precluded me from
reaching out for help. Instead, I proudly insisted on
doing things my way. I shoved my feelings under the
carpet when I appeared in public and perpetuated the facade that I was living the life of a joyful, happy person.
Behind closed doors I was miserable. By November I withdrew from the public eye except to fulfill commitments I
couldn't avoid. In mid-November I flew to Vero Beach,
Florida, to spend Thanksgiving with my folks and relatives. Although this change of scenery improved my emotional outlook somewhat, it only had a bandage effect on
the underlying problem.

The untreated wound of 1965, festering for 28 years,
now posed a dangerous health risk. The accumulating
emotional toxins began poisoning me, and my parents
knew something was definitely wrong. I lost my joy, and

the crazy sense of humor that characterized my unique personality disappeared. Always solicitous, they offered help. Something definite had to be done. No more temporary, quick fixes would work this time. Though grateful for their concern, I realized it was up to me, and me alone, to pursue a cure for my illness. I had to open up the wound and clean it out the proper way if I was ever to experience true healing. But who would perform the surgery? Knowing what was best for me, God used a gifted, sensitive and insightful counselor I'd worked with years before.

GLIMMER OF HOPE

In December, I returned to Cleveland after my three-week respite in Florida. Within minutes of entering the house, I telephoned Dr. Barnett Elman, the human emotional heart surgeon God assigned to my case. He wasn't in, but I was assured he would return my call.

Minutes later the telephone rang.

"Hello, Barnett. Thanks for getting back to me so promptly. Do you remember me from several years ago?"

"Of course. What can I do for you?"

"I need to talk to you."

"When?"

"Yesterday."

"That sounds pretty serious."

"It is."

"Is tomorrow afternoon soon enough for you?"

"Yes."

"Fine. I'll see you then. Good-bye."

Hanging up the phone, still miserable, I nonetheless felt a little glimmer of hope peek through the black clouds of my depression. Perhaps God could now begin the final healing process and rid me of that darn elephant in the living room!

The next day I began a three-month personal counseling commitment with Dr. Elman, in addition to a six-week couples' counseling pact with Dan, in an attempt to improve our communication skills and hopefully save our crumbling marriage. The first week of meetings sailed by uneventfully. Carefully controlling my emotions and the topics of discussion, I felt safe.

Deciding it was time to delve beneath the surface and address the real issues at hand, Barnett switched counseling gears the second week. That's when I rebelled. My previously controlled anger flared in his office one day during a couples' session, and the cat finally leapt out of the bag. In a rage, I stomped out of his office, whereupon he, his staff, and the other patients in the waiting room experienced first-hand my volcanic anger. There had to be a reason for it, he concluded, and he promised himself to address the issue the next time we met.

Tail between my legs, I meekly entered his office the following week. "I'm sorry for storming out on you like I did, Barnett."

"Don't worry about it. What exactly happened that caused you to react as you did?"

"I think Dan said something that pushed one of my buttons."

"What do you mean? Please explain."

THE ELEPHANT REVEALED

Thus started my narrative concerning the Cape Hatteras ordeal of 28 years before. With the story's telling, the never-addressed elephant in the living room revealed itself at long last.

"Have you ever expressed your feelings over what happened to you?" Barnett inquired.

Minutes passed. I sat there quietly, at a loss for words. I honestly didn't know what to say.

Finally I admitted: "I've never really thought about how I feel concerning what happened. No one ever talked to me about it when I was young. Everyone just avoided the topic and hoped I'd forget about it in time. As an adult I visited the Rape Crisis Center once. The counselor pointed out that I could have been killed during the rape and encouraged me to feel grateful I was still alive. Alive physically but not emotionally, I longed for her to address my turbulent emotional situation, but she didn't. Disappointed and hurting as badly as when I entered, I left her office and never returned. Then a few years ago I walked forward at church and forgave the man who raped me. This helped a lot to arrest the nightmares. But obviously, that was still not enough."

Actively listening, and sensing this as an important moment, Barnett narrowed his probing. "Have you ever allowed yourself to express the anger connected with this incident?"

I instantly exploded like before, again to the surprise of my husband seated beside me. "I'm not angry!" As the words spewed forth from my mouth and I felt my blood pressure spike, I exposed the long-hidden elephant and saw the real me for the first time—an angry, pained, desperate woman. The realization that I had this monster within me was frightening.

Recognizing the emotional breakthrough, Dr. Elman remained silent for what seemed an eternity and merely exchanged an encouraging glance with my stunned husband who helplessly sat there sensing my agony.

Finally Barnett spoke. "Marlane, I have a homework assignment for you, should you choose to undertake it.

Let me warn you ahead of time that it will require a lot of hard work and emotional involvement, but I believe it will prove to be quite beneficial."

Warily I asked, "What is it, Barnett?" By this time, weary from the 28-year battle waging within my soul, I hungered for emotional freedom and happiness. "I'm willing to do anything you think will help me. I trust you."

With that word of assurance and faith, he laid out the plan. "I want you to write down everything you would say and do to the rapist—legal or illegal—were you to encounter him again. Be specific. Don't hold back any thoughts or feelings because you don't think they're in keeping with what a Christian should think, feel, and do. Just get them all out on paper and report back to me." With that, he ended the session.

CHAPTER 15

THE COTTER PIN

D an and I had scheduled a 10-day working vacation in Palm Springs, California, over the Christmas holidays that year, so I decided to wait until then to begin my homework assignment.

Initially it felt like Mission Impossible. *Where would I begin? What would I say?* As I sat poolside, fear suddenly gripped me, and second thoughts bombarded my mind. *Do I really want to dig up the past and uncover these long-hidden emotions?* But I trusted Barnett and his counseling abilities and, quite frankly, was sick and tired of being sick and tired, so I opened my notebook and began.

I first prayed and asked God for help in this difficult undertaking. Years of denial and suppression of my feelings had frozen my emotions to the point that I didn't know what I felt or even how to feel. Hardness of heart had suppressed all my tears, and I unconsciously had constructed a thick, impenetrable wall around my spirit to insulate me from further pain and hurt. Successful heart surgery necessitated tearing down this wall and accurately identifying my long-denied feelings. Where and how would I begin? Crying out for God to speak to me, I sat still and waited.

Minutes melted into hours. Nothing. I numbly stared at the jubilant children splashing lightheartedly in the pool with seemingly not a care in the world. Oh, how I longed to be like them.

For four hours I sat with my mind flying from subject to subject, yet unable to focus or even put my thoughts on paper. *This is useless,* I concluded and started closing my notebook when all of a sudden the floodgates of my emotions broke, tears overwhelmed me at times, and I couldn't scribble the flowing thoughts and pent-up feelings toward the rapist fast enough. I wrote:

1. I'm angry at you for taking away my virginity against my will.

2. I'm angry at myself for trusting you to be an honest, wholesome person, and you weren't.

3. I'm angry at myself for not being more assertive and stopping you, no matter what I would have had to do.

4. I feel sad for you. You felt so poorly about yourself and so out of control and lacking power in your own life that you had to force yourself on me to achieve that sense of personal control.

5. I feel embarrassed and angry. You used me as an object for your convenience and then discarded me as if nothing wrong happened.

6. I resent you. After you used me, you probably unemotionally forgot me and what you did to me. On the other hand, I have borne the scars of the experience for 28 years.

7. I feel sad this experience tainted my God-given healthy attitude towards sex.

8. I feel angry. You robbed me of my innocence and my happy, carefree childhood.

9. I feel sad and embarrassed at how I dealt with male relationships after the rape. Had you not raped me, the chances are very great I would have established healthier male and female relationships.

10. I felt afraid for 17 years after the incident and subsequently experienced vivid nightmares.

11. I feel sad this experience negatively affected my trust in men.

12. I feel hurt, angry, and betrayed. You didn't listen to me, value me enough as a human being, and respect my wishes and feelings, but just selfishly went ahead and did what you wanted anyway.

Thus ended my list of positive expressions of anger towards the rapist. My list of negative things I'd say or do to the rapist if I were to encounter him again included:

1. Swear at him
2. Castrate him
3. Kick him
4. Beat him
5. Shoot him in the groin
6. Overpower him in some way, take away his control, and make him hurt in the same way he hurt me

I relived the traumatic experience for nearly two days. I cried and for the first time felt the loss associated with it. I cried and analyzed my emotions and subsequent behaviors. I cried and mourned the life I could have lived were it not for the rape. And I cried and anguished over my faltering relationship with my husband.

84

Dan, emotionally estranged due to our marital strug-
gles and aware of the counseling homework assignment,
kept his distance. Retreating into my own world, I isolated
myself, ignoring the outside world. I focused every ounce
of energy I could muster on me and what I needed to do to
heal from within. During this emotional marathon, I ate
little, ignored all but the basic personal hygiene concerns,
and slept fitfully.

After two agonizing days of struggle, the internal battle
ceased. The intricate heart surgery I experienced had
gotten rid of the deadly emotional poisons within me so
they could do no more damage. Although completely exhausted, somehow I felt different—relieved, clean, free—
for the first time in a long, long time. Now my heart was
prepared to receive the next phase of the healing through
a stranger in a wheelchair named Bill Cotter.

THE STRANGER'S STORY

Resting poolside in a chaise lounge, I reflected gratefully on the overwhelming, life-changing events of the previous few days. A physically challenged older gentleman
distracted my solitude when he wheeled himself to the
side of the shallow end, locked his brakes, and cautiously
lowered himself into the pool. Getting his bearings, he
slowly edged himself around to the deep end and stopped
directly in front of my lounge chair. As he approached me,
I greeted him with a sincere "Hello," and then, before I
knew what I was saying, I asked him the following question: "Sir, when you tell your wife 'I love you,' what do you
mean?"

Instead of ignoring me or judging me as some freak, he
looked me directly in the eye, paused momentarily to
think, and then delivered the most beautiful soliloquy on

love I ever heard. I sat there, all ears, drinking in his emotion-filled words and thoughts. Interjecting some observations about the institution of marriage, he concluded with the sage remark: "It's not worth it to be at odds with your spouse. Life's too short."

Then, for no apparent reason, he shared a personal story. A few years earlier, doctors diagnosed Bill with Parkinson's disease and stenosis of the spine. Deteriorating health forced him to look for someone he could hire and groom who would eventually buy his insurance company. After much searching, Bill finally settled upon a young gentleman and hired him. Within a few weeks, though, Bill detected a problem and suddenly thought he had made a grave mistake. In Bill's estimation, this individual didn't have the needed skills to successfully run the business, so Bill set out to sever his employment. All of Bill's efforts to intimidate the young man into quitting failed. He stubbornly persisted. One evening Bill and the young man encountered one another at a party.

The young man said, "Mr. Cotter, I know what you're trying to do to me. You're trying to make my life so miserable that I'll quit your business. I want you to know, though, no matter how difficult you make life, unless you fire me, I won't leave because I'm committed to this business."

These words pierced Bill's heart. That's what he needed to hear. This young man's statement of commitment to the enterprise changed Bill's attitude towards him, and from that day forward, Bill invested all of his efforts into helping the young man succeed in his endeavors. With Bill's support, the young man flourished in the business and eventually purchased the insurance company.

As Bill completed his story, he looked at me compassionately. Tears welled in my eyes. Unable to speak, I nodded and smiled. Bidding me good day, he edged himself back to the shallow end where he painstakingly exited the pool and disappeared into the hotel.

A COMMITMENT

A remarkable revelation occurred in those brief moments of conversation with Bill. While he shared his story, God simultaneously personalized it to my life circumstance. As Bill spoke of his relationship with the young man, it was as if the Lord were saying to me, "This is similar to your relationship with Dan. When you married him five years ago, you made a commitment to stay by his side 'for better or for worse.' Those words slipped easily from your tongue on your wedding day. Madly in love, and with no apparent problems before you, you had no idea what 'for better or for worse' meant. Then the difficulties began. Instead of crying out to Me, you pridefully decided to handle the problems in yourself and your marriage alone. Without My help, things got worse; and without realizing it, your heart hardened towards your husband. A wall rose between the two of you, and you withdrew your spirit and commitment from him and the marriage. If you want to experience true healing, joy, and happiness, you need to recommit your heart and spirit to Dan and to the marriage."

Later that day, as Dan and I packed to head for Carpinteria, California, once again I encountered Bill Cotter. He, too, was checking out of the resort. Running towards his wheelchair in an attempt to speak with my angel one last time, I leaned down, kissed him on the cheek, and said, "Bill, you'll never realize what you said to me today. Thanks for being used by God." Looking at me, quizzically and misty-eyed, he nodded, smiled, and with a good-bye wave, disappeared from my life as miraculously as he had entered.

A New Pledge

The long drive to Carpinteria forever changed the course of our marriage. Two hours of uncomfortable silence into the journey, I finally spoke. "Do you remember that man in the wheelchair we met?"

"Of course. He was a wonderful gentleman," Dan remarked.

"Bill certainly was. I'd like to share a story he told me."

"Okay. I'm listening."

With that, I told the story of Bill and the young gentleman. My voice faltered momentarily during the climax of its retelling when I shared the part about "I am committed to this business." After concluding the story, I paused a few moments to reorganize my emotions and thoughts.

Then I continued: "As Bill told this story, I realized I needed to do something. Dan, from this day forward, I recommit my heart and spirit to you and our marriage. I promise no matter what happens, I'll never leave you. I'll stay with you for better or for worse. I love you and pledge this to you, January 3, 1994." Speechless, Dan reached over, took my hand, and squeezed it appreciatively.

From that day forward, our marriage deepened. Although all our marital challenges didn't magically disappear, knowing we were stuck with each other for life no matter what, we decided to put down our boxing gloves. Now we would try to work better together, help one another overcome weaknesses and character defects, and strive to walk together in an ever closer fellowship with our heavenly Father.

God humorously and sovereignly brought a stranger, Bill Cotter, into my life at just the right time to save our marriage from impending doom, and in so doing, taught me a most valuable lesson. Like a cotter pin in mechanics can be so crucial in holding everything safely together, safety and security in marriage depends on commitment. If this crucial part cracks or breaks, disaster or death can result, whether it's physical death or death of a relationship.

I vowed that day in Palm Springs to regularly perform a maintenance check on my cotter pin—marital commitment—so nothing will ever jeopardize this most precious, God-ordained relationship between my husband and me. Through hard work, flexibility, and compromise, we're learning to not sweat the small stuff like toilet seats. Nowadays, our seat has its ups and downs depending on the user. Today I can truthfully say, "For better, for worse until death do us part." Amen.

CHAPTER 16
KVELL

When I returned to Dr. Elman's office after our California trip, he could tell something had changed. "You look different. Sit down and tell me specifically what happened." Choosing a comfortable chair and casually plopping myself down, I proceeded to share the results of my homework assignment. *This isn't the same angry woman who stormed out of my office two weeks ago,* he thought, listening to the story unfold.

"You told me to write down everything I'd ever say or do to the rapist if I ever encountered him again," I began. "After two and a half days of reliving, crying, and discovering the hidden emotions I'd stuffed all these years, here's what I came up with." I took out my tear-stained spiral notebook and matter-of-factly rattled off each point inscribed on the pages. Barnett sat listening intently, not interrupting my train of thought, and watched my body language, clinically assessing my vocal inflections as I shared. Concluding my last point, I quietly closed my notebook and waited anxiously for his reaction.

It seemed like an eternity before he spoke. "It strikes me as odd," he observed, "that you're able to express such intense feelings with no display of emotion at all."

"If you were with me in Palm Springs those two and a half days, Barnett, you would have witnessed, up close and personal, all of those intense emotions I just reported to you. Thank goodness the resort was practically deserted, or someone might have thought I was losing it and carted me off to a loony farm! My tear-smudged pages attest that I did, in fact, get in touch with my emotions. As I honestly dealt with the hurt, pain, lies, deceptions, and disappointments caused by the rape, one layer at a time, an inner peace replaced the gnawing knots in my stomach. The tightness in my chest subsided, and I was able to breathe again. I don't know if it makes any sense to you at all, but this is exactly what happened."

"It makes perfect sense to me," Barnett smiled with satisfaction. He paused to reflect and then added, "Do you feel you need to do any role playing to deal with the anger issue or bring closure to any other emotion?"

"No. I feel very much at peace." Barnett could see that peace and knew a miracle of healing truly had occurred.

"Good. There is one last thing I'd like you to do. Close your eyes and envision yourself with the rapist one last time. This time you're in control. Describe to me this last encounter with him and tell me what it feels like."

Laying my head against the back of the chair, I closed my eyes, took a deep breath, and let my mind focus on the rapist. Within a minute or two I vividly saw myself with my rapist and described it to Dr. Elman. "I see Herb on the ground, face down. I've tied his hands behind him, and he's immobile. I'm standing over him with my foot on his back. Showing my arm muscles in a display of strength, I wipe my hands as if to say the problem is solved, and he can't hurt me or anyone else ever again. Then I turn and walk away without looking back."

Barnett let me quietly reflect on this final encounter and eventually asked, "How do you feel now, Marlane?"

"At peace. It's behind me and I can now get on with life. What a blessing to finally be free!"

We met the following week just to make sure all was well. At the conclusion of the session Barnett said, "You're done. You don't have to come back anymore."

"Thank you, Barnett. You helped me so much. God used you richly in my life."

"You did a lot of the work yourself." (I knew in truth it was team work: Barnett, the Lord, and I.) As I rose to exit his office for the last time, we shook hands and hugged. "I'm so happy for you, Marlane. The only word that comes to mind to express how I feel is *kvell*."

I cocked my head curiously and inquired, "What's that word mean, Barnett? I've never heard it before."

"Kvell's a Yiddish expression which means 'bursting with happiness and joy.'"

"That word perfectly describes how I feel as well! God bless you, and again thank you."

With that, my counseling sessions concluded.

Chapter 17
The Freedom of Forgiveness

Recommitting myself to our marriage, I hungered for a healthy physical, emotional, and relational intimacy with my husband, but one major stumbling block still stood in the way: my ongoing spirit of unforgiveness.

Years before, in my emotional prison of hatred and bitterness, I had desperately cried out to God. He miraculously enabled me to forgive the rapist and thus put to rest the unrelenting nightmares of the past. For some reason, though, I unconsciously refused to apply this same principle of forgiveness to other less grievous matters in my life.

As far back as I can remember, our family walked around on emotional eggshells. An unspoken rule existed: a happy family doesn't argue, disagree, or have conflicts with one another. TV shows like "Leave it to Beaver" perpetuated this unhealthy, unrealistic lie. Everyday home life had generally proceeded peacefully and uneventfully with little conflict except the normal sibling rivalry between my brothers and me. I rarely witnessed my parents raise their voices to one another in disagreement, discuss a subject of controversy, forgive one another, reach an equitable solution, and kiss and make up.

Instead, the usual scenario, which I witnessed as a child, unfolded like this: seemingly out of nowhere, my father blew up in anger, blamed everyone else except himself for the problem, and then clammed up and gave us the silent treatment, sometimes for hours, sometimes for days. Unable to read his mind, none of us—my mother, brothers, or me—knew exactly what prompted his volcanic outburst, irresponsible verbal lashing, or our subsequent punishment of silence and relational isolation. Eventually in time, without a word of explanation, confession, forgiveness, or repentance, Dad got over his temper tantrum, started talking to family members, and life returned to normalcy until the next incident. This dysfunctional pattern of conflict resolution, which I detested, unconsciously imprinted itself within my spirit, and I regrettably carried this behavior pattern into my adulthood and marriage.

With no role modeling of healthy communication skills from my family, I naturally gravitated towards doing what was familiar in the midst of conflict. When the first arguments of our married life occurred, I found myself blaming Dan for the problem, irresponsibly spewing hurtful words of death I really didn't mean (but in my pride wouldn't admit), and then clamming up. Regrettably, I gave Dan the silent treatment that, as with my father, often lasted days. I went even one step further: I physically removed myself from our bedroom, choosing instead to sleep upstairs until the conflict subsided.

As my father had done, I never resolved any of our disputes through mature communication. I simply didn't know how. Instead, I assumed Dan could read my mind and therefore knew how he'd hurt me. I waited for him to say he was sorry, ask for forgiveness, then kiss and make up. I subconsciously refused to accept responsibility for any of my actions. When Dan didn't behave according to my expectations, I raged even more. Eventually—sometimes days later—without ever saying I was sorry, I'd move my belongings back into our bedroom and try to resume our relationship where it left off before the argument. Each time the cycle repeated itself, it took a little longer to get back to normal, and Dan, not understanding what caused the outbursts in the first place, found himself walking on emotional eggshells. He feared saying or doing anything that would set me off again. Incident after ugly incident seriously wounded our relationship in time and subtly undermined our commitment to one another.

A NEW WAY OF LIVING

The counseling with Dr. Barnett Elman that led to my emotional healing and recommitment to the marriage also affected my attitude towards forgiveness. Once I'd resolved I would remain in the marriage no matter how difficult it became, I realized it would be in my best interest to do anything necessary to reestablish a healthy, peaceable relationship with my spouse. Barnett subsequently met with us, taught us communication and conflict resolution skills, and encouraged us to hold one another accountable for our words and actions. After 40 years of unaccountability, at first I thought this assignment a pie-in-the-sky proposition.

Step one came the afternoon I approached Dan, told

him I wanted to change, confessed I couldn't do it alone, and asked him for help. "Honey," I began, "you know I hate myself when in anger I say and do things I don't mean and end up hurting you and others. I'm asking you to help me break this vicious cycle and replace it with a healthier form of behavior. Would you be willing to help me?"

"What would you like me to do?"

"In the future when I start reacting in my old, sick way, don't sarcastically say, 'You're doing it again!' Instead, help me by calmly encouraging me and saying something like this: 'You asked me to help you and remind you the next time you start falling into your old behaviors. This is what I'm doing. You may want to stop, take a second, think of a healthier way to respond, and then do so.'"

Dan thought for a while about the proposition and then willingly offered his help. This accountability exercise accomplished several things. It forced me: 1) to take the personal responsibility I had disregarded for years; 2) to acknowledge that I did make mistakes; 3) to humbly admit I couldn't change by myself and needed help; and 4) to establish and maintain a relationship between my husband and me, no longer based on control and power plays but on mutual respect and personal regard for one another. For the first time in our six-year marriage we were on the same page trying to help each other grow, mature, and reach our full potential.

Obviously, the first time I regressed into my past unhealthy behaviors and needed redirecting, Dan called me into accountability with fear and trembling. He didn't know whether I truly meant what I said and prayed I wouldn't bite his head off when he did what I asked.

Surprisingly, his head stayed intact. In fact, after he lovingly helped redirect my actions in a more positive way, I actually thanked him several times for his intervention! In time (old habits die hard), I replaced my former, destructive habits with new ones. This, in turn, led to less marital conflict and more peace overall.

I remember the day I first admitted I was wrong and asked Dan for forgiveness. Looking at me in disbelief with his mouth agape, he looked as if he was going to have a heart attack.

"I never thought I'd ever hear those words come out of your mouth. Congratulations and welcome to the real world!" he commended.

Ironically, I experienced a sense of relief when I transparently admitted my mistake and asked for forgiveness. The action cleared the air between us and allowed us to reestablish our intimacy with one another. This action also reestablished intimacy and a new-found transparency with my heavenly Father. Through humility, confession, and repentance, the thick walls of pride and unforgiveness fell. I surprisingly experienced the true freedom of forgiveness. What awesome freedom it is!

CHAPTER 18

A STONE'S THROW

I'd love to report a trouble-free, anger-free, conflict-free life since the day I exited Dr. Barnett Elman's office, but that wouldn't be true. Despite the human counselor's wisdom and guidance, real victory over anger didn't occur until I fully embraced the truths and principles (learned from both Barnett and the Bible) and practiced them repeatedly!

I humbly share two major setbacks to illustrate the saying, "Practice makes progress, not perfection." Thankfully, God is more patient with me than I am with myself. Every time I relapse into old behaviors, then admit I was wrong and ask Him to conform me more into His likeness, He forgives me, lifts me up out of the pit, dusts me off, and gives me a new chance. God's first such rescue occurred quite early after my emotional healing.

GOD'S RESCUE

It was April, nearly a month after I completed counseling. Mom, Dad, and I were eating dinner in their Florida winter home the night before Dad returned to Cleveland due to an emergency with their northern home. My father habitually videotaped a TV program, and early that day asked who would tape the show in his absence. Mom and I informed him that he could teach us how to program the machine, and we'd assume the duties. VCR illiterates ourselves, we asked what we thought a logical, intelligent request to ensure success in our endeavor on his behalf: write down the steps needed to accomplish the task, starting with step one, locate the TV. Since Dad didn't object to our request for written instructions, we assumed he'd comply and supply them before his departure.

Life progressed smoothly among the three of us the remainder of the evening until approximately 11:15 p.m. when my dad commented, "What about the VCR?" to which we reminded him of our request to write down the step-by-step instructions. Instantaneously, World War III erupted. Shouting like a drill sergeant and waving his hands in disgust, he retorted, "I don't have time to write down the instructions!"

"Well, is there an instruction manual I could read?" I innocently inquired.

Without thinking, he demeaningly snapped back, "You won't understand that. I guess we're going to miss all of the shows while I'm gone." He stomped out of the room adding, "She's never wanted to learn anything." Unwilling to let it go and allow emotions to cool, I stubbornly followed him into the bedroom and intensified the conversation.

"First of all, who's *she*?"

"Your mother," he groused.

"What do you mean, 'Never wanted to learn about anything'? What's *anything*?"

"Oh, about the VCR. I always do it."

"There you go again with your generalizations: 'She never does this or always does that.' It's not true, and it's not fair. You always say things like this! Why don't you grow up, Dad!"

Feeding on each other's heightened emotions and irresponsible words, we continued the verbal battle. Each of us hoped to claim victory in the winless skirmish. I resorted to reason once more and again requested he take us through the steps of setting up the VCR.

"It doesn't matter whether you know how to program the VCR anyway!" he barked.

Fed up with the whole miserable encounter, I stormed from his bedroom. Slamming his door behind me, I steamed into my room. My blood boiling, my heart pounding, I took a deep breath and replayed the mental and emotional tape of what just transpired. Ignoring my part in the argument and focusing only on my dad's inappropriate behavior, I smugly concluded, "Boy, is he immature!"

I disrobed, slipped under my bedcovers, folded my hands, and self-righteously prayed, "Thank you, Lord, for my father and all of his character defects." My eyes closed, and I reflected judgmentally on his many sins, when all of a sudden my eyes burst open, I sat bolt upright in bed and cried out, "Oh, my God! Look what I've become!" Without consciously realizing it, I had acquired the many character defects I so loathed in my father. Even though I'd just recently received an emotional healing, I inadvertently let down my guard and reverted to all of my old, unhealthy ways of handling conflict. "Lord, please forgive me," I repentantly prayed.

Getting out of bed, I donned my robe and walked into the living room in search of my father. "Dad, I'm so sorry for the way I behaved. Please forgive me." Without a word, he hugged me forgivingly and sent me off to bed with a clear conscience.

Lying in bed once again, this time praying with a humbled heart, I suddenly recalled a scripture pertinent to the evening's events: "He who is without sin cast the first stone" (John 8:7). Convicted of my own sin, I put down my stones, rolled over, and fell peacefully asleep. Like father, like daughter: I, too, was guilty.

CHAPTER 19

IT ISN'T OVER TILL IT'S OVER

Yet another time the elephant of anger and control, which I naively thought forever conquered, reared its ugly head, this time with Dan on a Sunday morning.

The words of the song "I Have Decided to Follow Jesus" still reverberated in my brain (but not my heart) as I resentfully pulled into the driveway alone after singing during two services at church. Slamming the car door behind me and defensively wielding my Bible and choir folder, I loudly stomped into the house. After deliberately dropping them on the kitchen table with a thud, I dramatically traipsed across the hardwood floor, high heels clanking, straight into the bedroom to change out of my church clothes and into my swimsuit. Pouting, I angrily walked from room to room in search of the object of my displeasure—Dan. Unsuccessful in my hunt, I decided to get a quick bite of lunch and continue the search outdoors. After all, he'd most likely be outside basking in the beauty of the hot summer day. Armed with my arsenal of literature on how to be a good Christian witness, I piously walked out to the pool, set up a chaise lounge, and sat down to study. (Truth be told, I emotionally donned my boxing gloves and eagerly awaited a verbal battle with my husband.)

There I sat for nearly 20 minutes, reading but not really reading. Instead, I fumed inside and schemed how I'd act when I first laid eyes on Dan. *It's show time!* I thought, as the din of the approaching lawn mower announced the arrival of my unsuspecting husband.

I adjusted my mirrored sunglasses, buried my head in the reading material, and ignored Dan's invasion into my quietude. Circling the periphery of the pool area, deftly steering the riding mower and intently focused on his lawn manicuring task, he didn't notice me at first. Three passes around the pool later, he finally caught sight of me, drove in my direction, shut down the engine, and smiling innocently, walked towards me with a sincere greeting: "Hi, honey! Were you sitting there all along?"

Perched on top of my cloud of piety and feeling "holier than thou," I curtly answered, "Yes."

"I didn't even see you."

"You really missed a good service."

"I know; they're always good," he agreed.

"What happened?"

"I told you I had a surgery case. By the time I was finished, I realized it was too late to get to church."

"You could have gone to the second service."

"I know."

"Yeah, you chose coming home and doing yard work as a higher priority than going to church!" I spouted.

My rising anger and the self-righteous tone of my voice

alerted Dan to back off and let the air clear. For the first time in two and a half months, I experienced the awkward feeling of alienation as I withdrew my spirit from my husband. Without taking time to assess my attitude and actions, I arose from my chaise lounge, grabbed my armload of reading material, and set up camp in a different part of the yard far away from him. There I continued my silent treatment temper tantrum for over an hour, despite the fact that, within minutes of my departure, Dan came over to my new venue, set up a chair two feet from mine, and plopped himself down so I couldn't miss him. Stubborn, I persisted in my old, silent ways until the internal simmering volcano of anger finally erupted, and all of the old, negative habits I thought I'd conquered, again gushed forth unbridled.

"I feel angry and hurt you didn't come to church today and hear me sing," I raged. "I can't believe it was more important for you to get your work done around the house than go to church. You never do things that are important to me. Remember last Thursday? I couldn't believe you were late in getting ready for that dinner engagement after we clearly discussed what time we had to leave home in order to get there on time. You knew how important the dinner was to me. When you ask me to accompany you to a dinner, I'm always on time, but you're never on time for me. And you didn't even apologize for being late last Thursday!" I lashed out as I pelted him with as much past garbage as came to mind.

"Yes, I did."

"No, you didn't."

"You're making those generalizations again, Marlane: 'You never; I always.' They're not true."

"Well, most of the time, then."

"You're trying to control me and make me go to church!"

The truth slapped me in the face. Prideful and determined to have the last word, I lied. "No, I'm not!" My temper flared as I picked up my beach towel, twisted it into a rat tail, and hoping for a reaction, smacked his swimsuit clad buttocks. Holding back snickers of laughter, I emptied my ice water bottle onto his unsuspecting prone torso and gloated as he squirmed uncomfortably on his chaise lounge. Then I defiantly spouted, "You can do all of the yard work today. I don't feel like doing it. It's not a priority to me." Getting in one last dig as I headed for the house, I vindictively announced, "And by the way, you can make your own dinner tonight." Predictably, Dan didn't follow me into the house and risk another verbal attack. Instead, he stayed outside and sunned himself until the clouds encroached.

Alienated from my best friend by my own choosing, I stood alone in the kitchen, feeling lonely indeed. *What in the world have I done?* I suddenly felt mortified by my behavior and mustered the courage to stop, breathe deeply, and take an inventory of what just transpired. Replaying the memory tapes of this nightmare, I focused on the words, "You're trying to control me." As I objectively evaluated the accuracy of his statement, I concluded Dan was right.

When he thought the dust had settled, Dan came into the house to change out of his swimming trunks and put on his work clothes. I followed him into the bedroom closet. Convicted of my total responsibility in the fiasco, I finally accepted it, and for the first time in a long time, didn't try to rationalize my actions. I simply said, "You were right. I was trying to control you. I have no right doing that. I was wrong. Please forgive me."

Stunned by my words of confession, he immediately came over and put his arms around me. He looked me in the eye and responded: "I forgive you, and I love you." I melted in his embrace. Instantly the emotional and physical walls of estrangement vanished and our spirits and minds reunited. Minutes later, reconciled and once again light-hearted, I donned my work clothes and willingly cut the remainder of the lawn, washed the mildewed aluminum siding, and joyously prepared a homemade spaghetti dinner for my love.

Progress At Last

Just what happened? First of all, I was caught off guard. Pleased with our marital recommitment, healthier communication and conflict management skills, and re-discovered love for one another, I naively thought the work concluded and we'd live happily ever after. In reality, though, when I rested on my laurels, complacency and pride were able to undermine our new marital foundation. After two brief months of new-found marital bliss, hairline cracks appeared. The Bible clearly states, "Pride comes before a fall" (Proverbs 16:18), and this incident accurately demonstrates it.

Two characteristics distinctly differentiate this experience from our many conflicts in the past—awareness and humility. This time I more rapidly recognized the dynamics of the conflict, took ownership for my responsibility in the problem, humbly admitted my sins, and asked for forgiveness. Dan, in turn, extended his grace and granted forgiveness. Through this challenge, we poignantly discovered the myriad blessings of applying these God-given life principles to our marriage. Practice does make progress!

CHAPTER 20

CAGED AT LAST

What about the elephant in my living room? I identified it as rape and subsequent unresolved anger. Present within my living room, invisible to me, but obvious to everyone else for more than a quarter of a century, this elephant impeded me from the emotional freedom and true joy God intended. Through the healing power of the heavenly Father, and in His perfect timing, I caged that menace and seized control of it. How? Through three things: recognition, admission, and humility. I finally recognized the need for help, admitted I couldn't do it on my own, and humbly asked for assistance from the One who was willing, waiting, and wanting to help. Through the healing process I learned valuable communication and life principles I now apply in the everyday challenges and trials of life so I can deal with conflicts immediately and thus live victoriously.

Though caged, my elephant—anger—is still very much

a part of me and always will be. Until I breathe my last, he will anxiously be looking for any opportunity to overpower me again and create a zoo of my life. This awareness that "It isn't over till it's over" keeps me humble, teachable, and coachable to God and His counsel in the Word. The Bible says, "Until now you have not asked for anything in my name. Ask and you will receive, and your joy will be complete" (John 14:26). Today I have joy! I have peace! I have victory! No more Dr. Jekyll/Mr. Hyde! No more volcanic eruptions! (Just an occasional lava flow.) Yahoo!

Although I lament the years spent in emotional bondage due to my denial and my lack of humility, I rejoice that victory is finally mine. Better now than never! As I daily turn my life over to the guidance of the Father (and it is a daily decision), He helps me control my elephant so it rarely causes an emotional ruckus anymore.

I've learned from personal experience that no problem's too great for the Master to solve. How encouraging and hopeful! As long as I have breath, I will glorify, love, and live for the One who taught me how to really live!

CHAPTER 21

YOU'RE INVITED!

So, my friend, what's the elephant in your living room? Anger, abuse, alcoholism? Whatever its name, you can have victory over it. Nothing is impossible with God! Perhaps you're searching for peace, joy, and fulfillment, but no matter what you do, where you go, or what you buy, you continually come up short. The uncomfortable, gnawing void in your heart and life remains. If this is the case, I invite you to try what I tried. It worked for me, and I know it will work for you. What do you have to lose?

The healing in my life began when I decided to have an ongoing, personal relationship with the Lord. Then, for the first time in my life, I could call upon the God of the Universe to help me and know, beyond a shadow of a doubt, that He not only heard me but would come to my aid.

Are you enjoying the fellowship of this relationship? If

so, I rejoice with you. If not, I invite you to contemplate what you've read in the previous account of my life and then decide if you'd like what I have.

We are all children of God. The heavenly Father desires us to experience intimate, transparent, meaningful fellowship with Him on a daily basis so He can help us overcome our personal elephants, whatever they may be.

A Personal Invitation

If you would like to take a step of faith and establish a personal relationship with the Lord:

1. Admit your need. (I am a sinner) [Romans 3:23]
2. Be willing to turn from your sins. (repent) [Acts 3:19]
3. Believe that Jesus Christ died for you on the cross and rose from the grave. [Romans 10:9-10]
4. Through prayer, invite the Lord to come into your heart, begin a daily walk with you, and establish an ongoing fellowship with you. [Revelation 3:20; John 1:12; Galatians 5:16-17]

Pray this simple prayer of faith:

"Dear Lord, I know that I am a sinner and need your forgiveness. I believe that You died for my sins. I want to turn from my sins. I now invite You to come into my heart and life. I want to trust and follow You as Lord and Savior. In Jesus' name. Amen."

Sign on the line, confirming your step of faith:

_____

signature   *date*

On the other hand, you may have given your life to the Lord years ago but, for some reason, have drifted away from an intimate fellowship with Him. He is waiting for you to rededicate yourself to Him. He bears no grudges, so you need not fear shame or ridicule as you reapproach His throne of mercy. His outstretched arms are ready to welcome you home!

Reach out to the Lord today, my friend, and His "Amazing Grace" and unconditional love will transform your life. You'll never be the same again! Amen and amen.

SPIRITUALLY FIT

Throughout my swimming competition years I craved victory and the sense of personal accomplishment and heightened self-esteem that accompanied it. Considering my coaches to be god, I trusted them implicitly and obeyed their every word of instruction. Since they willingly invested so much of their time and effort in me, I realized I owed it to them to do my utmost no matter the pain or sacrifice. Riveting my eyes on the goal, I refused to give up as I strove for excellence.

Now my competitive swimming days are but a memory; nonetheless, I still continue to exercise several valuable disciplines and regimens as I pursue my next goal: "One thing I do: Forgetting what is behind and straining toward what is ahead, I press on toward the goal to win the prize for which God has called me heavenward in Christ Jesus" (Philippians 3:13-14). In this spiritual race I'm running, I've developed the following daily regimen to keep me in shape:

1. As soon as I awaken, before I even get out of bed in the morning, I do the following:
   A. Say good morning to God
   B. Thank Him for a great night's sleep and the gift of a new 24 hours to live for Him
   C. Invite Him into my heart and life for the day and ask Him to guide and direct my footsteps, words, and actions
   D. Ask for God's protection so I can confidently and boldly face the day's events
2. After greeting my husband with a sustained hug and

kiss, I pour myself a cup of steaming hot, black coffee, and Dan and I congregate around the kitchen table to have our quiet time.

A. Holding hands, we first come before God in prayer and earnestly ask Him to open our spiritual eyes to discover all He knows we need to glean from His instruction book for the day.

B. Only then do we open the Word and read the scheduled Bible chapters for the day. Taking time to discuss unclear verses or study maps and instructional notes, we digest what we're reading and try to find practical application for our lives.

C. We spend quality time in prayer implementing the ACTS principle:

   1) Adoration: praising God for who He is: Savior, Lord, Master, Friend, Provider, Great Physician, Counselor, etc.

   2) Confession: confessing our sins to God—acts of commission as well as omission

   3) Thanksgiving: thanking Him specifically for the many things He's done in our lives

   4) Supplication: bringing our various needs and prayer requests to Him

D. After Dan leaves the table to get on with his day, I remain behind to just wait on the heavenly Father and listen to His still, small voice. Sometimes I sit quietly for five minutes, sometimes 15 minutes or more before I make the move to begin my day of scheduled activity.

It took 11 years of praying before my husband agreed to read the Word and pray with me on a daily basis, but I'm so grateful I didn't lose heart and quit. Now this priority time of intimacy with one another and the Father is the highlight of our day!

3. Sometime during the day I take time to get physical exercise. In my case, I normally swim a mile at the local pool. This isn't only healthy physically but it's also great spiritually. While mechanically swimming the 72 lengths, I oftentimes commit scripture to memory, sing praise songs in my mind and lift up prayer requests.

4. Finally, I daily commit to go beyond my comfort zone and sacrificially serve God in word and deed. It's not always easy. Some days I feel more spiritual than others and thus more willing to:

    A. call an ornery, negative former neighbor and take her shopping

    B. allow someone with a lighter load of groceries go before me in the checkout line

    C. share a word of appreciation with an impatient checkout clerk

    D. run an errand for a friend even if it's not convenient

Many times in my humanness I don't feel like being a reflection of God, especially when I'm tired or if I have other agendas on my plate. Experience is teaching me, though, that blessing and true joy will accompany every sacrificial act of kindness I do in His name, and my life will be more adventurous and exciting in the process.

5. Before I doze off to sleep at night, I thank Him for His great acts of love and faithfulness throughout the past day. If I have trouble falling asleep, I simply recite scripture, and before I know it, morning has dawned!

I don't follow this spiritual regimen perfectly every day although I try very diligently. If I mess up one day, I don't throw in the towel and quit. Instead, I confess my shortcomings to God, ask Him for motivation and perseverance the next day, put my failures behind, and get back in the saddle. After all, this relational fellowship with our heavenly Father is an ongoing daily journey, not just a one-time event. If the God of the Universe is willing to forgive me and love me unconditionally, then who am I to not forgive myself?

THE ELEPHANT HUNT

*Study questions for personal evaluation or
small group work created by Phyllis Ludwig
Zillmann and Marlane Zillmann Renner*

The following questions/personal inventory lists will help you identify any elephants in your life which are preventing you from really living. The success of your "elephant hunt" is dependent upon your honesty and transparency. As you venture into the "jungle" of your life, you may experience fear of what you'll discover. Take courage and know you're not alone. Hope, healing, health, and happiness await you! (Note: write your answers in a separate notebook.)

CHAPTER 1: THE ELEPHANT IN MY LIVING ROOM

Theme: Tragedy, problems, hurts, pain are part of life.

1. List the tragedies, problems, hurts, and pains you currently are experiencing or have experienced.
2. Describe the emotions you're feeling or felt associated with these problems.
3. Whom or what did you blame for these tragedies?

___God   ___another person
___circumstances   ___no one
___other (describe)_____

4. Explain how you have dealt with the tragedies, problems, hurts, pains listed in question #1.

5. Which tragedies, problems, etc., have you "buried under the carpet" and tried to avoid? Describe.

CHAPTER 2: YAHOO!

Theme: People don't like change. There's joy and satisfaction when we find our niche in life.

1. Write down the major changes you have had to make:
   ___career   ___place of residence
   ___relationships   ___death, separation, divorce
   ___other (explain)_____

2. My "Changeability" Barometer: Write down the statement that describes you best:
   ___I like change.   ___I dread change.
   ___I hate change.   ___I welcome change
   ___I'll do whatever I can to keep things just the
        way they are.

3. Explain how you dealt with each of the major changes you referred to in question #1.

4. Describe the value of being flexible, able to change rather than remaining rigid, resistant to change.

5. Have you found your niche in life? Yes or no. If yes, describe it.

CHAPTER 3: DR. JEKYLL AND MR. HYDE

Theme: We employ subconscious defense mechanisms to protect ourselves from being hurt again.

1. Describe the sensitive areas (issues) in your life.

2. What defense mechanisms have you constructed to keep you from getting hurt again?

3. What are your emotional "buttons"?

4. Who are the people in your life who seem to be good at "pushing your buttons"?

5. How do you respond/react when someone "pushes your button"?

6. Recall an incident when your reaction/response was inappropriate. Rewrite the scenario with the way you wish you would have responded.

CHAPTER 4: THREE STRIKES AND YOU'RE IN

Theme: Everyone needs to be loved unconditionally.

1. Do you believe in a higher power? Yes or no. If yes, describe what you believe.

2. Does what you believe satisfy your needs? Yes or no. If no, what seems to be missing? Explain.

3. What kind of relationship with a higher power do you desire? Describe.

4. Are you satisfied with your relationship with your higher power? Yes or no. If no, what changes do you need to make to improve your relationship? Describe.

5. What does "unconditional love" mean to you?

6. Is there anyone in your life who epitomizes "unconditional love"? Yes or no. If yes, name the individual(s).

7. Describe how the individual(s) show you unconditional love.

8. Who do you wish would show you unconditional love?

9. How do you wish this individual would show you unconditional love?

10. Do you show unconditional love to others? Yes or no. If yes, how? Describe.

11. Who is the role model of unconditional love in your life?

CHAPTER 5: HIS WILL, NOT MINE

Theme: There is great blessing in discovering God's life plan and choosing to walk in it.

1. What is your will for your life?

    A. Describe it by writing down your 1) plans 2) dreams and 3) goals.

    B. Write down your wants and desires in relation to the following areas:

    material   relational   emotional   educational
    spiritual   professional   sexual   physical

    C. Write down your needs in relation to these areas:

    material   relational   emotional   spiritual

2. List major decisions you made that worked out well.

3. List major decisions you made that in retrospect were mistakes and led to disappointment.

4. List major decisions you made in haste which you later regretted.

5. List major decisions you made that you hadn't really planned but in retrospect turned out better than you ever dreamed.

6. Do you believe God has a plan for your life? Yes or no. If yes, what do you believe His plan is for your life? Describe.

7. What vehicle(s) does God use to express His will/plan for your life?

    ___prayer   ___Bible
    ___counsel of other people   ___song
    ___newspaper/magazine article
    ___sermon/inspirational message
    ___other_____

8. Have you ever received a "message" from God? If so, what was it? How did you receive it?

9. Describe the benefits of discovering and walking out God's plan for your life.

10. Describe the disadvantages of walking out God's plan for your life.

11. Do you trust God to do what's in your best interest for your life? Yes or no. If no, why not?

CHAPTER 6: HOOVER

Theme: Weight problems and eating habits are inextricably linked to our emotional health and sense of well being.

1. "Food for Thought": Write down all that apply:

___I live to eat!

___I eat to live.

___I reward myself with food.

___I console myself with food.

___I feel guilty when I eat things I know I shouldn't.

___At times I lose control when eating.

___I've lost and gained hundreds of pounds over the years.

___I am currently in control of my eating.

___I am currently out of control of my eating.

___I like what I see when I look in the mirror.

___I don't like what I see when I look in the mirror.

___I don't care about what I see when I look in the mirror.

___I use my weight as a defense mechanism to protect me from getting too close to others and possibly getting hurt

___I have been discriminated against by others because of my weight.

___I feel good about how much I weigh.

___I would like to weigh less. (What would you like to weigh?)

___I would like to weigh more. (What would you like to weigh?)

___I consider my weight a factor in whether or not I'm loved by others.

___If I weighed less, people would love me more.

2. Describe how you feel when you are in control of your eating.

3. Describe how you feel when you are out of control of your eating.

4. Have you ever pictured how you would like to look? Describe it.

5. Recall a time when you were out of control in your eating. Describe your emotional health at that time. What was happening in your life which could have triggered your eating binges?

6. "Sense of Well Being" Barometer: Which statement accurately describes you at this point in your life?

___I am content, confident, comfortable with who I am

___I am not happy with who I am

___I wish I were someone else

7. Identify other areas of your life in which you struggle with self control.

___alcohol   ___work
___sex   ___sports
___exercise   ___shopping
___gambling   ___other_____

CHAPTER 7: IS HE THE RIGHT ONE?

Theme: We often experience a heart "tug of war," a desire to be loved but "on my terms." Past relational hurts make us gun shy, controlling, and cautious. Our biggest fear is being hurt all over again.

1. Describe your personal fears regarding relationships.

2. List any past hurts in relationships that still haunt you today.

3. Have you or are you dealing with these past hurts? Describe.
4. Describe a hurt in a past relationship which made you gun shy and afraid of getting hurt again.
5. If married, did you marry someone who reminded you of your father/mother? Yes or no.
6. "Control" Barometer: Write down the statement that best describes you.

___I am a controlling person.
___I let other people control me.
___I see myself as a victim of others' control.
___I resent people controlling me.
___I want to have more control of my life.
___I feel comfortable with myself and don't allow others to control me.
___other_____

CHAPTER 8: MT. ST. HELENS—WATCH OUT!

Theme: We often hide behind a facade of perfection and peace and only reveal the "real" self (the good, the bad, the ugly) to those closest to us.

1. "Who am I?" Write down all statements that apply.
___I am a transparent person.
___I often hide behind a facade, afraid to reveal my true self to others.
___I am afraid that if people saw the real me, they would not like me.
___I can not stand the thought of not being liked. I need to be liked by everyone.
___At times I say or do things contrary to my beliefs in an effort to be accepted by others.
___I know who I am.
___I haven't a clue who I really am.

___I don't want to know who I really am.
___I like myself.
___I don't like myself.
___I accept myself.
___I don't accept myself.
___I condemn myself.
___I hate myself.
___I love myself.
___I've contemplated doing away with myself.

2. Have you ever said or done something to hurt the one you loved the most? Yes or no. If yes, describe one incident that comes to mind.

3. How long ago did that incident occur?

4. Do you have any regrets concerning this incident? Yes or no. If yes, what were they?

5. How would you have acted differently if you could relive the experience? Describe.

6. List the people who seem to be the "ones you hurt the most."

7. List the people who hurt you the most.

CHAPTER 9: YOUR AD DIDN'T LIE

Theme: God has a creative, humorous way of introducing us to our future spouse, and it's always in His perfect timing.

1. List the character traits important to you in the "ideal" spouse.

2. Have you ever met "Mr./Mrs. Right"? Yes or no. If yes, did you marry him/her? Yes or no.

3. Questions for married individuals:
   a. Describe how you met your spouse.
   b. How long did it take you to find "Mr./Mrs. Right"?_____
   c. After you met "Mr./Mrs. Right," how long did it

take you to discover he/she was "Mr./Mrs. Right"?_____

   d. Did you ever try to make "Mr./Mrs. Wrong" "Mr./Mrs. Right"? ___yes ___no If yes, what were the consequences?

   e. Have you ever doubted whether your spouse was "Mr./Mrs. Right"? ___yes ___no

CHAPTER 10: A LIFETIME OF ADVENTURE

Theme: Disappointments can lead to new adventures.

1. Are you married? Yes or no.
2. Have you ever been married? Yes or no.

   ___separated   ___divorced   ___widowed

3. Describe several adventures you experienced with your spouse.

4. Describe a deferred plan/trip/dream which in the end turned out to be a positive adventure of a different kind.

5. "Marriage Barometer": If you are currently married, how would you describe your marriage? Write down all that apply.

___exciting	___boring
___sedentary	___adventuresome
___spontaneous	___unimaginative
___wild	___romantic
___dull	___dead
___growing	___mature
___complete	___ "business deal"
___convenient	___compatible
___combative	___argumentative
___battlefield	___peaceful
___abusive	___loving
___supportive	___pathetic
___nurturing	___encouraging

___draining   ___negative

___other_____

6. If not married, would you like to get married? Yes or no. Why or why not?

CHAPTER II: "LEAVE AND CLEAVE"

Theme: Marital problems ensue if parental ties are not severed prior to marriage.

1. When you got married, did you sever parental ties and cleave to your spouse?

   ___yes, before my marriage started

   ___yes, but only after problems cropped up in the marriage

   ___no

2. Describe several marital problems that arose because parental ties were not broken prior to marriage.

3. List advantages of severing parental ties.

4. List disadvantages of severing parental ties.

5. "Spousal Loyalty" Barometer: Write down all statements that apply to you.

   ___I complain about my spouse to my parents.

   ___I'm guilty of tearing down my spouse in front of others.

   ___My girl friends/male friends know about my marital problems.

   ___I keep private issues in my marriage private.

   ___I respect my spouse.

   ___I do not respect my spouse. Explain why not.

   ___I love my spouse.

   ___I do not love my spouse.

6. How do you show your spouse you love him/her?

7. What is your spouse's "love language"?

8. How do you think your spouse would complete this

125

statement: "If you loved me, you would..."?

9. Complete the following statement: "My spouse can show me he/she loves me by..."

10. "Communications" Barometer: Evaluate your communications skills with your spouse.

___excellent
___adequate
___something to be desired
___lacking or nil

11. Have you ever had marital counseling? Yes or no. If yes, describe how it either made matters better or worse.

12. "Listening" Barometer: Write down all statements that apply.

___I am a good listener.
___I am a poor listener.
___My spouse is a good listener.
___My spouse is a poor listener.
___I wish my spouse would listen to me.
___It hurts me when my spouse does not listen to me.
___When communicating with my spouse, I find myself thinking about what I'm going to say when he/she stops talking, and therefore I don't really hear what is said.
___I need to learn new listening skills.
___Listening is an important part of communication and an integral part of a healthy marriage.

13. Have you ever threatened to leave home? Yes or no.

14. Did you ever leave home? Yes or no.

CHAPTER 12: THE FALL GUY

Theme: It's human nature to blame others rather than accept personal responsibility for our actions. Unresolved problems from the past poison current relationships and situations.

1. Do you have a "fall guy" or scapegoat, someone or something you blame rather than accepting personal responsibility for your words or actions? Yes or no. If yes, write down all who are or have been a "fall guy" in your life.

___spouse   ___friend
___relative   ___neighbor
___stranger   ___children
___in laws   ___boss
___co-worker   ___ex-girl/boy friend
___former spouse   ___the dog/cat
___wealth/poverty   ___destiny
___luck   ___God
___the devil   ___weight
___other_____

2. Does it help to blame someone else? Yes or no. Explain.

3. Has blaming someone else ever backfired? Yes or no. If yes, explain.

4. "Personal Responsibility" Barometer: Write down the statement which applies to you.

___It's hard for me to accept personal
     responsibility for my actions.
___I'm comfortable accepting personal
     responsibility for my actions.
___I tend to try to blame others for my actions and
     only accept personal responsibility when I'm
     "pressed to the wall."
___I've never explained to my "fall guy" what
     he/she does to "push my emotional buttons."

5. Describe any unresolved issues from the past that are poisoning current relationships.

6. Describe the emotions that well up inside of you when you think of the unresolved conflict or issue.

7. In what areas of your body do you feel the effects of this unresolved conflict?

___stomach   ___head

___neck   ___back

___other_____

8. Do you have any physical ills that can be attributed to this unresolved conflict? Write down all that apply.

___depression   ___insomnia

___nervousness   ___ulcers

___hypochondria   ___other_____

9. Explain what YOU can do to resolve the conflict.

10. Explain the disadvantage of waiting for the other person to take the first step in resolving the conflict.

11. Is the person with whom you have an unresolved conflict living or dead?

CHAPTER 13: ROCK BOTTOM

Theme: We often need to come to the end of ourselves, hit rock bottom, before we're ready for emotional healing.

1. Have you ever hit rock bottom? Yes or no. If yes, describe what it was like.

2. How did you know it was rock bottom?

3. Did you isolate yourself from other people? Yes or no.

4. Did you contemplate suicide? Yes or no.

5. What steps did you take to get out of rock bottom? Describe.

6. Is "rock bottom" how you would describe your life right now? Yes or no. If yes, have you told anyone you know that this is how you are feeling? Yes or no.

7. When you are feeling "low," who is the person in your life with whom you feel comfortable to share your inner hurts and pains? Name the person.

8. Is there anyone you know who appears to be at rock

bottom in his/her life right now? Yes or no. If yes, what have you done to offer help? Describe.

9. Do you know anyone who has attempted/committed suicide? Yes or no. If yes, who?

10. Describe the effect the suicide had on loved ones, friends, co-workers, etc.

11. Did you blame yourself for the person committing suicide? Yes or no.

12. List people/organizations/hotlines which could offer assistance to individuals experiencing emotional "rock bottom."

CHAPTER 14: MISSION IMPOSSIBLE

Theme: Healing begins when we courageously, truthfully address the real problems that lie beneath the surface which are often masked by seeming other "problems."

1. "Problems" Barometer: What problems are you facing? Write down all that apply. Make two lists—one for primary and one for secondary problems in your life.

___work	___relationship w/spouse
___children	___temper/anger
___relation w/in-laws	___gossip
___obesity	___pride
___low self esteem	___alcoholism
___natural disaster	___bankruptcy
___loss of a dear friend	___loss of spouse
___no purpose for life	___feeling of uselessness
___bitterness	___gambling obsession
___retirement	___health problems
___aging	___loss of child
___divorce	___relocation
___loneliness	___boredom
___infidelity	___war memories

___rejection   ___abandonment
___relation with parents   ___other_____

2. Are you motivated to work on one of the problems you identified above? Yes or no.

3. Choose one problem you are currently experiencing. Describe it in detail.

4. Brainstorm what steps you can take to remedy it.

5. Would outside resources/organizations/counseling, etc., be helpful in resolving the problem? Yes, no, or possibly. If yes, list some resources you would feel comfortable using in helping to resolve your problem.

6. How would resolving this problem help resolve some of the other problems you are facing?

CHAPTER 15: THE COTTER PIN

Theme: God uses other people often times to speak truth to us.

1. List people in your life whose opinions you respect.

2. Describe an instance where one of these people was a "lifesaver" in your life (helped you when you really needed help).

3. Did you recognize it at the time? Yes or no.

4. Did you ever recognize retrospectively that someone was a "lifesaver" for you? Yes or no. If yes, describe the incident.

5. Have you ever refused help from someone? Yes or no. If yes, why? What happened as a result of your refusal to accept help? Describe.

6. Do people ever call you and ask for help? Yes or no.

7. Are you willing to help others in need? Yes or no.

8. Give an example of when you were in the "right place at the right time" to help someone in need or receive help yourself. Describe the incident.

9. Do you believe in angels or those whom "God sends"?
Yes or no.

CHAPTER 16: *KVELL*

Theme: Final resolution to problems produces joy!
1. Describe a problem you were finally able to overcome.
Explain how you felt.
2. Did that success inspire you to tackle another problem
in your life? Yes or no. If yes, what was the next problem
you decided to tackle? Explain.
3. Did you share your success with someone else whom
you knew cared about you? Yes or no. If yes, what was
that person's reaction to the good news? Describe.
4. Are you currently "weighed down" by a problem you
would like to overcome? Yes or no. If yes, what is it?
Explain.

CHAPTER 17: THE FREEDOM OF FORGIVENESS

Theme: Bad habits learned from previous generations can
be broken with conscious effort and accountability.

1. "Forgiveness" Barometer: Write down all that apply.
___I am emotionally "free."
___I harbor unforgiveness towards others.
___I am bitter because of unforgiveness I have
   towards others.
___I can't forgive myself.
___I keep a score of offenses committed against me
   and feel compelled to get even.
___Getting even gives me satisfaction.
___I hate myself when I retaliate.
___I'm repeating the bad habits of my parents.
___I feel justified in harboring unforgiveness.
___I feel tied up in knots.

___I want to forgive, but I just can't bring myself to
do it.

___There are some things I just can't forgive.

2. Describe an area of unforgiveness you are currently
battling.

3. Describe how forgiving will make a difference in the
situation. What are the advantages to forgiving? What are
the disadvantages?

4. Recall an incident where you forgave someone for of-
fending you. Was the person you forgave aware that a
problem existed? Yes or no.

5. What was the person's reaction when you forgave
him/her? Describe.

6. Is any physical problem you've been having better as a
result of your act of forgiveness? Yes, no, or I don't know.
If yes, explain.

7. Is there anyone in your life holding you accountable
for your words and actions? Yes, no, or I don't want to be
held accountable for my words and actions. If yes, who is
your "accountability" person? If no, would you like
someone to hold you accountable for your actions and
words? Yes or no. If yes, who would you like as your "accountability" person?

8. Explain the advantages of having someone in your life
to hold you accountable for your words and actions.

9. Explain the disadvantages of having an "accountability" person in your life.

CHAPTER 18: A STONE'S THROW AND CHAPTER 19: IT ISN'T OVER TILL IT'S OVER

Theme: "Practice makes progress, not perfection."
Relapses are normal when we try to break old habits.
Awareness, humility, and forgiveness lead to healthier
living.

1. List any habits you have which you would like to break.
2. Describe the consequences of having these habits.
3. From whom did you learn the habit? Was it passed down from a previous generation? Yes or no. If so, what can you do to prevent it from being passed down to yet another generation? Explain.
4. What steps can you take to break them?
5. Are there any bad habits in your life you have had success in breaking? Describe.
6. Did you experience a relapse in the process of trying to break it? Yes or no. If yes, how long did it take you to "get back in the saddle" after the relapse?
Are you still experiencing relapses? Yes or no.
7. Whom did you blame for the relapse?
   ___self　　　___others
   ___situation outside of your control
   ___other_____
8. Did breaking one bad habit lead to starting another bad habit? Yes or no. If yes, explain.
9 If you are currently battling a bad habit, what's keeping you from experiencing victory over this habit? Explain.
10. How can you eliminate these "roadblocks" to victory over the bad habit? Explain.
11. What is your motivation for breaking the bad habit? Is it a valid motivation? Yes or no.
12. List the advantages of breaking the bad habit.
13. "Perfectionist" Barometer: Write down all that apply.
   ___I am a perfectionist.
   ___I am not a perfectionist.
   ___I set a goal for overcoming all of my "character defects" and when I fail to meet my goal, I feel like a failure.

___I am persistent.
___I give up easily.
___I'm my own worst enemy.
___I accept myself "warts and all."
___I can excuse my own humanity.
___I'm no worse than anyone else; after all, times
    have changed.
___other_____

CHAPTER 20: CAGED AT LAST

Theme: "Caging" our elephants, whatever they may be, is a daily discipline and decision.

1. List the "elephants" you have identified in your life.
2. Have any of them been "caged"? Yes or no. If yes, explain.
3. Describe your plan of action for caging your elephant on a daily basis.
4. Has this book given you any useful tools to implement in caging your elephants? Yes or no. If yes, describe.
5. Have you achieved freedom over your elephant? Yes or no. If yes, has it given you the encouragement and incentive to hunt for other elephants in your life? Yes, no, or I'm not ready to hunt for elephants at this point in my life.
6. If you have experienced freedom over your elephant, answer these questions:
    a. At what point did you become sick and tired of being sick and tired and decide to do whatever it took to cage your elephant? Describe.
    b. Describe what it feels like to be free of your elephant.
    c. Would you recommend this freedom to others? Yes or no.
    d. Has anyone close to you seen a difference in you as a result of caging your elephant? Yes or no.

e. Would you say your efforts were worth it? Yes or no.

APPENDIX: "SPIRITUALLY FIT"

Theme: A disciplined life physically, spiritually, and relationally keeps us in shape as we run the race of life.

1. Do you lead a disciplined life? Yes or no.
2. Describe your daily routine.
3. "Physical Exercise" Barometer: Write down the statement that best describes your exercise discipline.

    ___I exercise daily.

    ___I exercise 3-4 times per week.

    ___I exercise once a week.

    ___I exercise only when I feel like it.

    ___I never exercise.

4. "Spiritual Exercise" Barometer: Do you have a disciplined spiritual life? Yes or no. If yes, write down all that apply.

    ___I read spiritual material daily.

    ___I meditate daily.

    ___I pray daily.

    ___I attend a place of worship on a regular basis.

5. "Relational" Barometer: Write down all that apply.

    ___My relationship with my spouse/significant other is healthy.

    ___My relationship with my spouse/significant other is not what it could be.

    ___My relationship with my children is good.

    ___My relationship with my children is strained.

    ___I have healthy relationships with friends.

    ___I am a loner and don't have friends.

    ___other_____

6. Discipline Evaluation: Write down the statement that best describes how you feel.
___I don't feel I need to make any changes in my life.
___I need to make changes in my life.
7. Describe what changes you need to make in the following areas:
Physical exercise:
Spiritual exercise:
Relationships:
8. Describe the plan you will undertake to make these changes.

MAY GOD BLESS YOU AS YOU PURSUE A
SIGNIFICANT BREAKTHROUGH IN YOUR LIFE!
HAPPY HUNTING!

The author has made a commitment to pray for a breakthrough in the lives of the readers of this book. If you would like to share your specific prayer request or testimony of how God has used this book in your life, please write the author at the address below.

Send your prayer request, testimony, or request for information about speaking engagements to:

Marlane Z. Renner
P.O. Box 731, Gates Mills, OH 44040-0731
e-mail: mrenner@core.com
www.there-is-hope.com

PUBLISHER'S GUARANTEE
If you are unhappy with the purchase of this book,
you may return it directly to the publisher
(address at front of book) for a full refund.